TREES
&
SHRUBS

© AA Media Limited 2011
Written by James Hall

Produced for AA Publishing by D & N Publishing, Baydon, Wiltshire

Commissioning editor at AA Publishing: Paul Mitchell
Production at AA Publishing: Rachel Davis

Printed and bound in China by C&C Offset Printing Co. Ltd

A CIP catalogue record for this book is available from the British
Library.

ISBN 978 0 7495 6831 3
    978 0 7495 6853 5 (SS)

The contents of this publication are believed correct at the time of
printing. Nevertheless, the publishers cannot be held responsible
for any errors or omissions or for changes in the details given in this
guide or for the consequences of any reliance on the information
provided by the same. This does not affect your statutory rights.

Published by AA Publishing, a trading name of AA Media Limited,
whose registered office is Fanum House, Basing View, Basingstoke,
Hampshire RG21 4EA. Registered number 06112600.

A04089
theAA.com/shop

CONTENTS

Trees are almost always the largest living things in any British landscape, but we frequently see them only as a green backdrop to whatever is happening in the foreground. Their characteristics as individual, beautiful and fascinating living plants can too easily be overlooked. But trees are much more than lovely objects: they provide essential habitats for wildlife, as well as valuable shade and shelter, and they help to keep us alive by recycling carbon dioxide into oxygen.

Traditionally managed woods are immensely rich in wildlife.

The *AA Spotter Guide to Trees and Shrubs* covers 182 species. The list includes all the native and widely naturalised trees and shrubs you are likely to encounter on a regular basis in the British countryside at large – in woods, hedgerows and scrub areas. Additional species have been selected on the basis of their interest in the context of gardens, parks and ornamental plantings. Overall, there is an emphasis on trees rather than shrubs, as these have the most obvious impact in the landscape.

A full page is devoted to each species. The text has been written in a concise manner so that as much information as possible can be provided in the space available. Each species entry begins with the common English name and is followed by the species' scientific name. For ease of use, the subsequent text has been divided into sections: **FACT FILE**, which covers the species' size, habitat preferences, flowering period and habit (its overall appearance and growing style); **IDENTIFICATION**, which describes its appearance in more detail, giving information about leaves, flowers and bark in particular; **STATUS AND COMMENTS**, which describes where the species occurs in Britain, and provides an indication of its abundance or scarcity; and **KEY FACT**, which gives further information on the species in question, often as an aid to identification, or provides facts that illuminate the species' origins, uses or special characteristics.

There are surprisingly few native British trees. Experts differ on the total, the number varying between 35 and 60 or so, depending on definition, opinion, and continually changing scientific nomenclature. In this book, we have attempted to say whether trees and shrubs are native, introduced or naturalised, but it is often a grey area and one that changes as a result of new discoveries and re-assessments of past assumptions.

Why so few natives? Essentially, the reason is because what we now call Britain was scoured by successive ice ages, then isolated from mainland Europe by seas, preventing recolonisation after the ice receded.

But today in Britain, if you work hard, you can track down thousands of different kinds of tree, and very many more different shrubs, introduced by man. Some – such as certain trees that have edible fruit, the Cultivated Apple being a good example – were introduced so long ago that no one really knows when or by whom. Others, such as Sweet Chestnut, were probably introduced by the Romans. The vast majority, however, are recent introductions, brought here in the last few hundred years, particularly during the great age of botanical collecting in the 19th and early 20th centuries. It is to intrepid plant hunters such as David Douglas (1799–1834), Robert Fortune (1812–80) and E.H. Wilson (1876–1930) that we owe so many of the trees and shrubs that now seem to be so at home here.

Some of the trees and shrubs in this book are 'man made'; that is they are hybrids created by deliberately crossing one plant species with another. Such plants (normally identified by the '×' in their scientific name) cannot really be said to be native to anywhere. Other hybrids may occur in the wild.

What is the difference between a tree and a shrub? In this book a 'tree' is usually described as a plant that normally achieves a height of more than 3m; shrubs tend to be smaller and often have no pretensions to 'treeness', such as a single main trunk or distinct crown. It is, however, a grey area: some of the willows, for example, are tiny but 'feel' like trees; and Hazel can grow to 7m and more, but do its multiple stems make it a very large shrub rather than a tree?

Britain may not have many truly native trees and shrubs, but the ones it does have are vital for wildlife. Our oaks are the most famous in this respect, supporting hundreds of species of insect, and possibly hundreds of thousands of individual insects on a single tree. Trees are also frequently home to mosses and lichens, some of which are confined to particular species in particular areas. Many of our butterflies depend on trees, shrubs and woodland for habitat and for food. Among these are the spectacular Purple Emperor, White Admiral and Silver-washed Fritillary.

Trees once covered much of the British landscape, but man has adapted virtually every landscape in Britain, with perhaps only the tops of the highest mountains and the most remote sea cliffs now remaining truly 'wild' and unchanged. Trees have long been vital to man's survival – for firewood, for building shelters, for making tools and even for food. But people also needed open areas for growing crops and keeping livestock, so vast swathes of woodland were cleared. Those that remained were intensively managed for wood and timber for many different purposes, but, remarkably, the management regimes that were developed and that remained virtually unchanged until the 20th century were actually beneficial to much of our wildlife. Traditionally managed woodland is the place to go if you want to see those magnificent butterflies mentioned above, for example, and it is in such woodlands that the best displays of spring flowers are frequently found. Why? Because the traditional management regimes were based on patterns of clearance and renewal, and upon maintaining a variety of species at a wide variety of ages and stages of growth. The supposed benefits of monocultures of conifers (now discredited) created woodlands that were deserts so far as much wildlife was concerned. The neglect since the end of World War II of much of our once-managed woodland that escaped coniferisation has led to declines in wildlife of all sorts.

So, if you want to help Britain's trees and its wildlife, join one of the County Wildlife Trusts (www.wildlifetrusts.org) and/or the Woodland Trust (www.woodlandtrust.org.uk), and perhaps go out on a working party to help re-establish Britain's ancient, incredibly rich woodland habitats. But at the very least, get out there and enjoy our wonderful trees and shrubs.

Calcareous Soils containing calcium, usually derived from chalk or limestone.

Catkin Hanging spike of tiny flowers.

Clone A plant derived asexually from a single plant (for example, by means of cuttings or suckers) and genetically identical to that plant.

Columnar Rather narrow and erect.

Conifer A cone-bearing tree.

Coppice A plant cut down nearly to the ground to encourage a growth of new young shoots.

Cultivar Short for 'cultivated variety'; a plant created in, or selected for, cultivation.

Deciduous Having leaves that fall in autumn.

Evergreen In leaf throughout the year.

Hybrid A plant that is the result of the cross-fertilisation of different species.

Introduced Non-native.

Involucre Ring of bracts (modified leaves) surrounding a flower or flowers.

Lanceolate Narrow and lance-shaped.

Leaflet One of the divisions of a compound leaf.

Lenticel Breathing pore (often warty) on a trunk, branch, stem or fruit.

Lobe Projection on a leaf (larger than a tooth).

Native Not known to be introduced.

Needle Narrow leaf of a conifer.

Palmate Leaves with finger-like lobes arising from the same point in a hand shape.

Pinnate Leaves with opposite pairs of leaflets on a central stem.

Pollard A plant cut down to a short bole, from which new branches grow.

Sepal Outer segment of a flower, outside or behind the petals.

Stipule Leafy appendage at the base of a leaf stalk.

Stub Plant base, often very woody and sometimes ancient; the result of coppicing.

Sucker Shoot arising from roots, possibly eventually forming a new plant.

Tooth Small projection on the margin of a leaf.

Variegated Leaves with different coloured patches.

Variety A recognised variant of a species.

MAIDENHAIR TREE
Ginkgo biloba

SIZE **Height to 40m** HABITAT **Parks, arboretums, botanic gardens** FLOWERS **Apr–Jun** HABIT **Slender, with one trunk; slightly conical when mature. Deciduous**

IDENTIFICATION

Leaves have unmistakable fan shape with at least one deep incision; 10–12cm long; dark green, turning yellow and gold in autumn. Flowers and fruits are rarely seen in Britain. Fruits are up to 3cm long; unpleasant smell when ripe.

STATUS AND COMMENTS

In Britain, you are most unlikely to see this native of China outside of cultivation. Young trees are inclined to be wispy and undistinguished apart from the leaves, but mature trees are handsome and impressive.

KEY FACT

Maidenhair Trees are either male or female; the female carries the oval fruit, inside which is a single seed. Most British trees are male.

SPOTTER'S CHART

LOCATION	DATE/TIME

COMMON YEW
Taxus baccata

FACT FILE SIZE **Height to 25m** HABITAT **Woodland, hedges, gardens, churchyards** FLOWERS **Feb–Apr** HABIT **Varied, from an upright single stem to hunched, gnarled, many-stemmed. Conifer**

KEY FACT Every part of the Common Yew is poisonous; even crushing the leaves can be dangerous. Birds can eat the sticky red fruits because they expel the deadly stone undigested. Keepers of livestock are especially nervous of the species.

IDENTIFICATION
Leaves are up to 30mm long, borne singly on both sides of shoot; dark green and leathery. Flowers are tiny, yellow, borne along stem; male trees release clouds of pollen in early spring. Fruits are red blobs, appearing from late summer. Bark is red-brown.

STATUS AND COMMENTS
Widespread native. In some S counties it occurs in single-species woods – strange, dark, magic-seeming places. Really ancient Yew trees are most often seen in churchyards.

SPOTTER'S CHART

LOCATION	DATE/TIME

MONKEY PUZZLE
Araucaria araucana

SIZE Height to 30m HABITAT Parks, arboretums, gardens, botanic gardens FLOWERS May–Jul HABIT Mature trees have a tall, single trunk, with most branches towards crown. Conifer

IDENTIFICATION
Leaves are spiny, dark green, carried in a tight array on stem. Both male and female trees produce cones, those of female up to 17cm long. Bark is thick, wrinkled and frequently scarred. Branches are often slightly drooping. Very distinctive and unlike any other tree in Britain with its prickly, spine-laden branches.

KEY FACT
The Monkey Puzzle became popular immediately upon its introduction to Britain at the end of the 18th century. It has often been planted in seemingly unlikely places, including suburban gardens.

STATUS AND COMMENTS
Native to South America, where it is now rare; seen sporadically throughout Britain, sometimes in town gardens. Its unique appearance makes it stand out.

SPOTTER'S CHART

LOCATION	DATE/TIME

FACT FILE   SIZE Height to 40m in Britain HABITAT Parks,
gardens, hedges FLOWERS Mar–Jun HABIT Columnar;
the numerous forms adopt many shapes and sizes. Conifer

IDENTIFICATION

Leaves are tiny, scale-like, carried
on flattened sprays. Distinctive
squarish pea-sized cones take
a year to develop. Bark is red
to purple. Trunk may be
many-branched. A good aid
to identification is the scent,
which some liken to parsley.

KEY FACT   The large
number of varieties began to
appear of their own accord
shortly after the tree was
introduced to Britain in 1854.
They are all said to retain the
parsley-like scent.

STATUS AND COMMENTS

Native to North America, where
it is now rare, but it can be seen
in its many forms throughout
Britain. A popular garden tree,
with several variants from yellow
to dark green, and from upright
to weeping.

SPOTTER'S CHART

LOCATION	DATE/TIME

NOOTKA CYPRESS
Chamaecyparis nootkatensis

FACT FILE

SIZE Height to 30m in Britain **HABITAT** Parks, gardens
FLOWERS Mar–May **HABIT** Mature trees are tall, elegant and
conical, with neat, drooping branches from ground to crown. Conifer

IDENTIFICATION
Leaves are very small, scaly, carried in flattened sprays. Bark is grey
to orange; stringy to touch. Branches are typically elegantly drooping.
Has a pungent scent some find
unpleasant. Varieties are
uncommon but do occur.

KEY FACT When mature,
this is a very handsome tree that
is as elegant and tidy inside the
canopy as out. In its native forest
habitat it can be incredibly
long-lived.

STATUS AND COMMENTS
Introduced to Britain from **NW
USA** in 1854. Not a common
tree, and unlikely to be seen
on calcareous soils.

SPOTTER'S CHART

LOCATION	DATE/TIME

LEYLAND CYPRESS (LEYLANDII)
× *Cuprocyparis leylandii*

SIZE Height to 30m **HABITAT** Parks, gardens, hedges **FLOWERS** Often none, but sometimes May–Jul **HABIT** Often seen as a large hedge; mature trees are tall and conical. Conifer

IDENTIFICATION
Leaves are small and scaly, often carried irregularly on sprays. Bark is reddish brown with vertical ridges. Dense, very fast-growing habit. Its numerous cultivars include the more robust 'Leighton Green' and yellowish 'Castlewellan', along with the aptly named 'Haggerston Grey'.

STATUS AND COMMENTS
If ever a tree could be called ubiquitous, this is it. Leyland Cypress is a hybrid (hence the vigour) between Nootka Cypress and Monterey Cypress, and first appeared in parks in Britain in the late 1800s.

KEY FACT
Its immense vigour makes Leyland Cypress a popular hedging plant – and the cause of many boundary disputes when it becomes out of control. Its thuggish ways can be tamed if the tree is kept tightly trimmed.

SPOTTER'S CHART

LOCATION	DATE/TIME

MONTEREY CYPRESS
Cupressus macrocarpa

FACT FILE

SIZE Height to 40m HABITAT Parks, gardens, often by the sea on S and W coasts FLOWERS Apr–Jul HABIT Young trees resemble skittles; spreading when mature. Conifer

IDENTIFICATION
Leaves are tiny and scaly, held stiffly on forward-facing shoots. Cones are up to 5mm across, with a point on each scale. Bark is greyish brown with wide vertical ridges. Mature trees have a spreading, aristocratic crown. Tree has a fresh, lemon-like scent.

KEY FACT
Monterey Cypress is now much more common in Britain than in its native range, where it is restricted to a few locations on the Californian coast near Monterey. It is salt- and wind-tolerant.

STATUS AND COMMENTS
A native of the USA, this cypress is more likely to be seen near the sea than inland, and is not usually grown in plantations. Varieties include the yellowy-gold 'Goldcrest', and 'Lutea'.

SPOTTER'S CHART

LOCATION	DATE/TIME

ITALIAN CYPRESS
Cupressus sempervirens

FACT FILE

SIZE Height to 40m **HABITAT** Some parks and gardens **FLOWERS** Mar–May **HABIT** Typically a tall, thin column, especially cultivars such as 'Stricta'; others are spreading. Conifer

IDENTIFICATION

Leaves are very small and dark green. Bark is dark brown with wide vertical ridges. Trees are usually seen as a narrow column of foliage, including the very thin cultivar 'Green Pencil'. Usually dark green, but 'Swane's Gold' appears yellow. Often has no detectable scent.

STATUS AND COMMENTS

Elegant and formal, the Italian Cypress is most likely to be seen in parks, gardens and landscaped cemeteries in Britain, where it is not very widespread. It is native to the S Mediterranean area as far E as Iran.

SPOTTER'S CHART

LOCATION	DATE/TIME

KEY FACT

In some Mediterranean countries this tree is more widely planted than any other.

INCENSE CEDAR
Calocedrus decurrens

FACT FILE

SIZE Height to 40m **HABITAT** Parks, gardens
FLOWERS Nov–Jan **HABIT** Variable; often a tall column
when mature; often skittle-shaped when young. Conifer

KEY FACT
The tree's common name comes from its distinctive aroma, said by some to be like turpentine or polish. It is said to be easy to raise from both seeds and cuttings.

IDENTIFICATION
Leaves are tiny scales up to 3mm long, held in pairs on sprays. Young cones are distinctive – yellowy, almond-shaped and 2.5cm long; old, open cones are browny yellow. Bark is reddish brown with scales and plates. Whole tree is aromatic.

STATUS AND COMMENTS
Native to the **NW** coast of the USA, this is a popular tree, planted in Britain much more widely now than previously, partly because of its resistance to disease.

SPOTTER'S CHART

LOCATION	DATE/TIME

FACT FILE SIZE Height to 7m HABITAT Uncommon; mostly on chalk in S; pine woods in Scotland; limestone in N FLOWERS Mar–May HABIT Variable, from prostrate to upright shrub. Conifer

IDENTIFICATION

Leaves are small and needle-like, with a white band on surface; carried on stem in whorls in groups of three. When mature, cones look like small, dark blue fruits and are very aromatic, as is the whole plant. Bark is reddish brown and often peeling.

KEY FACT

Common Juniper 'berries' are used to flavour gin (some say the plant smells of gin) and in cooking. The dense wood is used in woodcarving and was once widely used to smoke foods.

STATUS AND COMMENTS

Common Juniper is one of Britain's three native conifers. It has suffered a decline as its preferred habitats – such as chalk downland – have disappeared.

SPOTTER'S CHART

LOCATION	DATE/TIME

DROOPING JUNIPER
Juniperus recurva

FACT FILE

SIZE Height to 15m **HABITAT** Occasional parks, gardens **FLOWERS** Mar–May **HABIT** Mature trees have drooping branches, a dense appearance and often dead foliage. Conifer

IDENTIFICATION
Leaves are small and needle-like, held in whorls of three, with two white bands on underside. Cones resemble those of Common Juniper; aromatic, but less pleasant than Common Juniper cones. Bark is reddish brown and often obviously peeling.

STATUS AND COMMENTS
Drooping Juniper is native to the Himalayas and parts of China, and hence is sometimes called the Himalayan Juniper. There are two distinct varieties in its native habitat.

KEY FACT

Drooping Juniper is not often seen in Britain, where it is confined to larger gardens and parks. Some cultivars may have accentuated drooping characteristics.

SPOTTER'S CHART

LOCATION	DATE/TIME

WELLINGTONIA (GIANT SEQUOIA)
Sequoiadendron giganteum

FACT FILE

SIZE **Height to 50m in Britain** HABITAT **Mainly parks, large gardens, arboretums** FLOWERS **Feb–Apr** HABIT **Very tall, conical column. Conifer**

KEY FACT The few stands in California of this 'living fossil' include General Sherman, which at a height of 84m and trunk volume of 1,487cu m may be the biggest individual tree in the world. Some Wellingtonias are more than 3,000 years old.

IDENTIFICATION

Leaves are tiny scented spines. Bark is reddish and very spongy, and in mature trees develops massive buttresses on lower bole. Branches often begin many metres up; lower branches are swooping. Overall impression is one of massiveness and majesty.

STATUS AND COMMENTS

In its native habitat on the **NW USA** coast, this is one of the tallest trees in the world, growing to more than 80m. In Britain, the tallest is 52m.

SPOTTER'S CHART

LOCATION	DATE/TIME

COAST REDWOOD (COASTAL REDWOOD)
Sequoia sempervirens

SIZE Height to 50m in Britain **HABITAT** Arboretums, parks, large gardens **FLOWERS** Feb–Apr **HABIT** Stately and immense with a thin trunk; drooping, uneven branches. Conifer

FACT FILE

KEY FACT
Unlike most conifers, the Coast Redwood can regenerate from a fallen tree or felled stump. It is known equally as the Coastal, Coast or Californian Redwood.

IDENTIFICATION
Leaves are of two sorts: those on side shoots are 2cm long, rather like leaves of Common Yew and very different from those of Wellingtonia, with two white bands underneath; those on young stems are scale-like and up to 8mm long; scent of both is said by some to resemble grapefruit. Bark is reddish brown, very thick and fibrous.

STATUS AND COMMENTS
In its native habitat – a narrow coastal strip in California and Oregon – this species tops heights of 100m, making it one of the world's tallest trees.

SPOTTER'S CHART

LOCATION	DATE/TIME

SWAMP CYPRESS
Taxodium distichum

FACT FILE

SIZE **Height to 35m** HABITAT **Parks, arboretums, large gardens** FLOWERS **Mar–Apr** HABIT **Most often conical, but older trees may have rounded tops. Deciduous conifer**

IDENTIFICATION

Leaves are 1.5cm-long needles, carried on alternate shoots along stem; shed in autumn, when they may become burnished red. Bark is pale reddish brown, sometimes becoming grey.

STATUS AND COMMENTS

This native of E USA coastal areas and the Everglades was introduced to Britain in 1640 by plant hunter John Tradescant the Younger. It is most likely to be seen in S Britain.

KEY FACT

The humped and rounded 'knees' that develop in trees growing in wet (not dry) ground may help the trees to 'breathe' and also help retain valuable silts around the root area.

SPOTTER'S CHART

LOCATION	DATE/TIME

POND CYPRESS
Taxodium ascendens

FACT FILE

SIZE Height to 20m **HABITAT** Parks, arboretums, large gardens; generally confined to **S Britain** **FLOWERS** Mar–Apr
HABIT Smaller and slighter than Swamp Cypress. Deciduous conifer

KEY FACT
Not a common tree in Britain, and mostly seen in S areas, the Pond Cypress lacks the 'knees' of its close relative the Swamp Cypress.

IDENTIFICATION
Leaves are tiny (8mm), held on upward-pointing shoots; shed in autumn, when the tree may turn bright rusty red. Bark is reddish brown and may peel in strips. A very close relation of the Swamp Cypress, but its upward-pointing shoots are quite different.

STATUS AND COMMENTS
Like the Swamp Cypress, this tree is native to S and E USA, where it grows in swamps and wet places.

SPOTTER'S CHART

LOCATION	DATE/TIME

DAWN REDWOOD
Metasequoia glyptostroboides

FACT FILE SIZE Height to 30m HABITAT Parks, gardens FLOWERS Rarely flowers in Britain HABIT Slender cone when mature; immature trees have a looser outline. Deciduous conifer

IDENTIFICATION

Leaves are small and flat; pale green when emerging in spring, darkening later in year and turning red in autumn; carried on opposite shoots on stem. Bark is reddish, sometimes peeling in vertical strips.

KEY FACT

Seriously endangered as a wild tree in its native range, the Dawn Redwood became immediately popular and widely planted on its introduction to Britain and Europe. It is considered to be easy to grow and to propagate.

STATUS AND COMMENTS

This native of SW China (where it was not discovered until 1941) is a popular park and garden tree in Britain, and is sometimes confused with Swamp Cypress (note that it lacks 'knees').

SPOTTER'S CHART

LOCATION	DATE/TIME

WESTERN RED CEDAR
Thuja plicata

FACT FILE

SIZE Height to 50m in Britain HABITAT Parks, gardens, plantations FLOWERS Mar–May HABIT Mature trees are usually narrow and conical; cultivars may be more compact. Conifer

KEY FACT
The Western Red Cedar can grow to 65m and more in its native habitat; Britain's oldest specimens are still growing, having been introduced in the 19th century.

IDENTIFICATION
Leaves are tiny, flat and glossy; distinct pineapple scent. Very small brown cones dot the leaf sprays in autumn. Bark is reddish brown with fibrous ridges, these often forming buttresses at base of trunk.

STATUS AND COMMENTS
A native of NW USA. In Britain, it is as likely to be found in forestry plantations as it is to be found in parks and gardens.

SPOTTER'S CHART

LOCATION	DATE/TIME

FACT FILE SIZE Height to 20m HABITAT Occasional parks and gardens FLOWERS Mar–Apr HABIT Much like Western Red Cedar, but in Britain nearly always smaller. Conifer

KEY FACT The leaves of this species, also known as Eastern White Cedar and American Arbor-vitae (meaning 'tree of life'), were once eaten to combat scurvy.

IDENTIFICATION
Leaves are tiny, flat and scale-like, sometimes yellowish; their very aromatic, sharp scent is a clear aid to identification. Bark is orange-brown or grey. Has numerous varieties, none common in Britain.

SPOTTER'S CHART

LOCATION	DATE/TIME

STATUS AND COMMENTS
This native of E coastal USA may have been introduced to Britain as early as the 16th century, but it has never thrived here.

EUROPEAN SILVER FIR
Abies alba

SIZE Height to 50m HABITAT Most common in
Scotland FLOWERS Apr–May HABIT Younger trees carry whorls of
slightly upturned branches; older trees are often irregular. Conifer

IDENTIFICATION
Leaves are thick needles
up to 3cm long, with a
notched end and two
white bands underneath.
Cones are carried high
up in tree and often
disintegrate *in situ*.
Bark is grey to white.
In Britain, mature trees
often look weather-
beaten and may have
many broken branches.

KEY FACT
In its native
heartlands this is a real giant,
reaching as high as 70m. Known
as *Tannenbaum* to German-
speaking peoples, it is used as a
Christmas tree.

SPOTTER'S CHART

LOCATION	DATE/TIME

STATUS AND COMMENTS
A native of central Europe. Once
widely grown as a timber tree, the
European Silver Fir is no longer
planted commercially in Britain
as it is prone to aphid attack in
milder climates.

FACT FILE

SIZE **Height to 60m in Britain** HABITAT **Large gardens, arboretums, commercial plantations** FLOWERS **Apr–May** HABIT **Very tall and thin when mature. Conifer**

IDENTIFICATION

Leaves are long (5cm) and slender, arranged in two flat rows either side of stem; very distinctive, pleasant orangey scent. Bark is dark grey-brown. Mature trees are very tall spires with quite loose-looking, slightly upturned branches, carried all up the trunk, often to a widening top.

SPOTTER'S CHART

LOCATION	DATE/TIME

KEY FACT

The name says it all. In its native habitat the Giant (or Grand) Fir can grow very fast to heights of 80m.

STATUS AND COMMENTS

Not especially common in Britain, this native of **NW USA** and Canada often makes its presence felt by its sheer height – it can grow a metre a year, and British specimens have reached more than 60m.

DEODAR
Cedrus deodara

SIZE Height to 40m in Britain HABITAT Parks, gardens FLOWERS Rarely flowers in Britain; Aug–Nov HABIT Elegant and conical. Conifer

IDENTIFICATION

Leaves are needle-like, 2–5cm in length, and dark green with grey lines on either side. Bark is dark brown, becoming almost black in mature trees; has vertical plates. Branches have a slight but characteristic downwards turn at tip. Overall conical shape is often a good identification aid.

KEY FACT
In its native habitat the Deodar can reach heights in excess of 80m, but so far it has reached only half that in Britain.

STATUS AND COMMENTS

The Deodar, a Himalayan native, has been widely planted in Britain and continues to be popular here. Dainty young trees are often seen in smaller gardens, while handsome mature trees grace larger gardens.

SPOTTER'S CHART

LOCATION	DATE/TIME

FACT FILE SIZE Height to 40m in Britain HABITAT Parks, larger gardens FLOWERS Aug–Nov HABIT Usually keeps to a broadly conical shape into maturity. Conifer

IDENTIFICATION

Leaves are up to 2cm long, carried in clusters. Male (yellow) and female (green) flowers appear on same tree. Bark is dark grey; in mature trees comprises fissured plates.

KEY FACT

The Atlas Cedar is sometimes regarded as a subspecies of Cedar of Lebanon, from which it is often most easily distinguished by its growing habit.

Branches tend to be upwards-inclined and may become flat plates in mature trees, but not as pronounced as in Cedar of Lebanon.

STATUS AND COMMENTS

The species originates in the Atlas Mountains of North Africa. The variety most often encountered in British gardens is the Blue Atlas Cedar (var. *glauca*), with bright blue-tinged foliage.

SPOTTER'S CHART

LOCATION	DATE/TIME

CEDAR OF LEBANON
Cedrus libani

FACT FILE

SIZE Height to 40m HABITAT Parks, larger gardens, arboretums FLOWERS Aug–Nov HABIT Columnar rather than conical. Long branches with huge clumps of foliage. Conifer

KEY FACT
The Cedar of Lebanon grows much faster than its reputation suggests – remarkably so once it has become established.

IDENTIFICATION
Leaves are needle-like, up to 3cm long; usually carried in clusters, although long, new shoots carry single leaves. Bark is dark grey with ridges and fissures; mature trees have very dark brown bark. The great plates of foliage on long branches in open-grown trees are very distinctive.

SPOTTER'S CHART

LOCATION	DATE/TIME

STATUS AND COMMENTS
A native of the E Mediterranean. In Britain, huge old Cedars of Lebanon are emblematic of open lawns around stately homes and large country parks and gardens. Such trees often have massive fissured trunks.

FACT FILE

SIZE **Height to 40m** HABITAT **Commercial plantations, parks, gardens** FLOWERS **Feb–Apr** HABIT **Tall, straight, narrow and conical. Deciduous conifer**

IDENTIFICATION

Leaves are needles, up to 3cm long, carried in bunches at intervals on stems; bright green new leaves appear quite late in spring; in autumn, leaves turn brown or dusky gold and fall off. Bark is greyish brown. Often has dead branches complete with cones at any height.

KEY FACT

Its ability to grow a completely straight single trunk in a comparatively short time has made this a popular commercial tree, especially for posts and poles.

STATUS AND COMMENTS

A native of central Europe, the Common Larch is most often seen in Britain as a commercial forest tree, but is a good conifer for the garden as it casts only light shade.

SPOTTER'S CHART

LOCATION	DATE/TIME

JAPANESE LARCH
Larix kaempferi

FACT FILE

SIZE Height to 35m HABITAT Commercial plantations; occasionally parks and arboretums
FLOWERS Mar–Apr HABIT Conical and branchy. Deciduous conifer

IDENTIFICATION

Leaves are needles up to 3cm long (wider than those of Common Larch). Bark is reddish brown. Difficult to tell from Common Larch: Japanese has cream or pink female flowers, whereas in Common they are red; Japanese cone-scale tips turn back, whereas in Common they do not; Japanese may appear to be a more densely branched tree.

KEY FACT
This tree grows more vigorously than the Common Larch, its European counterpart. The heavy leaf-fall is welcomed by foresters as an undergrowth suppressant, but this reduces the biodiversity of the areas in which it grows.

STATUS AND COMMENTS

Native to Japan, the Japanese Larch in Britain is very much a tree of commercial plantations, where its thick leaf-fall in autumn can smother undergrowth.

SPOTTER'S CHART

LOCATION	DATE/TIME

HYBRID LARCH/DUNKELD LARCH
Larix × eurolepis/Larix × marschlinsii

FACT FILE SIZE Height to 40m HABITAT Almost exclusively commercial plantations FLOWERS Mar–Apr HABIT Fast growing, with a single straight main stem. Deciduous conifer

IDENTIFICATION
Leaves are very similar to those of both parents (Common Larch and Japanese Larch) but may be longer. Bark is reddish brown. Telling this hybrid from its parents is tricky at the best of times, and can be trickier still as the tree often reverts to either parent in appearance.

STATUS AND COMMENTS
This hybrid tree is quite widespread in plantations but difficult to distinguish from its parents. It goes by two English and two scientific names, and is a real test for the expert tree-spotter!

KEY FACT
More vigorous than either parent, this hybrid is popular with foresters for its ability to stand up to tough growing conditions.

SPOTTER'S CHART

LOCATION	DATE/TIME

NORWAY SPRUCE
Picea abies

FACT FILE

SIZE Height to 45m **HABITAT** Commercial plantations; in gardens often as a small tree **FLOWERS** Feb–Apr **HABIT** Mature tree is a very tall, thin spire. Conifer

IDENTIFICATION
Leaves are four-sided needles, up to 2.5cm long, with a sharp point; and dark green. Female flower is upright and red. Cone is a dark brown pendent cylinder up to 18cm long. Bark is reddish brown, darkening with age, often with resin patches. Plantation trees may have few, or dead, lower branches.

KEY FACT
The Norway Spruce can grow to nearly 70m in its native habitat. In Britain, its hardiness and popularity as a Christmas tree mean it is widely planted.

STATUS AND COMMENTS
This native of N Europe is the 'classic' Christmas tree. It is grown in Britain in huge numbers for that purpose and often subsequently planted out in gardens, where it looks conspicuously out of place.

SPOTTER'S CHART

LOCATION	DATE/TIME

SITKA SPRUCE
Picea sitchensis

FACT FILE

SIZE **Height to 60m** HABITAT **Commercial plantations in areas with abundant rainfall** FLOWERS **Mar–May** HABIT **Mature trees have a very tall, narrow cone shape. Conifer**

IDENTIFICATION

Leaves are flat needles, up to 3cm long, with two white bands on underside; very sharp. Female flowers are green. Cones are brown cylinders up to 10cm long. Bark is greyish brown, becoming purple. Large trees have a substantial trunk that may be buttressed.

KEY FACT This, the largest of the spruces, can grow up to 80m in its native habitat. In time, trees in Britain may also reach that height.

STATUS AND COMMENTS

A native of the **NW** coast of the **USA** and Canada, this is an important forestry tree and the most widely planted conifer in Britain. It does best in moist areas, and poorly in dry ones.

SPOTTER'S CHART

LOCATION	DATE/TIME

WESTERN HEMLOCK
Tsuga heterophylla

SIZE Height to 50m in Britain **HABITAT** Commercial plantations; also arboretums, parks, large gardens **FLOWERS** Apr–May **HABIT** Conical with dense foliage; can grow very tall. Conifer

IDENTIFICATION
Leaves are flat needles, up to 2cm long, dark green with two pale bands on underside. Bark is dark brown, becoming fissured with age. Trees can look very different depending on their situation: in ideal conditions they are a wide cone shape, but in dense, near-dark plantations are overbearing.

KEY FACT
This species is considered to be one of the most useful of all timber trees – its wood is used for a wide range of purposes, including paper production.

STATUS AND COMMENTS
A native of northern North America and widely planted in Britain as a commercial tree, the Western Hemlock does best in wet conditions away from calcareous soils.

SPOTTER'S CHART

LOCATION	DATE/TIME

EASTERN HEMLOCK
Tsuga canadensis

FACT FILE

SIZE Height to 25m HABITAT Parks, gardens; sometimes commercial plantations FLOWERS Mar–May HABIT Broadly conical, with drooping lower branches. Conifer

IDENTIFICATION

Leaves are small needles, up to 1.5cm long, tapering to a rounded tip; dark green with two white bands on underside; some are carried upside down on shoots. Cones are markedly small: up to 2cm long. Bark is reddish brown. Branches often touch the ground.

STATUS AND COMMENTS

A native of E Canada and the USA as far S as Alabama, the Eastern Hemlock is most likely to be encountered in Britain in parks and larger formal gardens. Its numerous cultivars have differing shapes and forms.

KEY FACT

The Eastern Hemlock is a much smaller tree than its relative the Western Hemlock. It has many cultivars, which often emphasise the drooping, ground-hugging habit.

SPOTTER'S CHART

LOCATION	DATE/TIME

DOUGLAS FIR
Pseudotsuga menziesii

FACT FILE

SIZE **Height to 60m in Britain** HABITAT **Commercial plantations; sometimes parks and larger gardens** FLOWERS **Mar–May** HABIT **Tall, narrow, conical, often with a loose-limbed outline. Conifer**

IDENTIFICATION

Leaves are small needles up to 3cm long, with two distinct white bands on underside. Ripe cones (up to 10cm long) have unique drooping, three-pronged bracts. Bark is purple-brown, often with resinous blisters. Tree is pleasantly aromatic.

KEY FACT

In its native habitat the Douglas Fir can grow to 100m. It is also known as Oregon Fir and Oregon Pine, and was introduced to Britain in 1827 by Scottish botanist David Douglas.

SPOTTER'S CHART

LOCATION	DATE/TIME

STATUS AND COMMENTS

A native of the W coast of North America, the Douglas Fir is a widely planted commercial tree in Britain, where it does best in moist conditions, particularly in Scotland.

SIZE **Height to 40m** HABITAT **Very widespread,
including mountains, moors, heaths, coasts; also parks and gardens**
FLOWERS **Apr–Jun** HABIT **Varied; often open-canopied. Conifer**

KEY FACT Scotland's surviving
original forest fragments and stands of
Scots Pine – the Caledonian forests
– are a unique habitat that contains
specialised wildlife. Restoration of some
of the remaining fragments is a
conservation priority.

IDENTIFICATION
Leaves are dark green
twisting needles, up to 7cm
long, carried in pairs. Cones
are egg-shaped, up to 7.5cm
long; green when young,
brown when mature. Bark
is reddish brown with a
papery surface.

STATUS AND COMMENTS
A British and European native, Scots Pine has also been widely planted.
It self-sows readily in the right conditions, and can become a nuisance.

SPOTTER'S CHART

LOCATION	DATE/TIME

LODGEPOLE PINE AND SHORE PINE
Pinus contorta

FACT FILE

SIZE **Height to 30m** HABITAT **Plantations**
FLOWERS **Apr–Jun** HABIT **Lodgepole Pine (ssp. *latifolia*) is tall and thin; Shore Pine (ssp. *contorta*) has a rounded canopy. Conifer**

IDENTIFICATION
Leaves of Lodgepole are up to 10cm long, broad, dark green, twisted, and carried in pairs on stem; Shore leaves are shorter, up to 7cm. Cone of Lodgepole is small (50mm); cone of Shore is longer (60mm). Bark is very dark brown in both. Mature Shore Pine has a broader, wider profile.

KEY FACT
In their native range these subspecies grow in very different habitats: Shore near the coast; Lodgepole always inland. Lodgepole Pine was used by Native Americans to build tepees, hence its common name.

SPOTTER'S CHART

LOCATION	DATE/TIME

STATUS AND COMMENTS
These two subspecies are natives of North America and have been widely planted in Britain. They make good growth on the poorest, wettest soils, and are weed suppressants.

FACT FILE   SIZE **Height to 40m** HABITAT **Plantations, shelter belts, parks** FLOWERS **Apr–Jun** HABIT **Often slightly asymmetrical in profile, becoming conical, then flat-topped with age. Conifer**

IDENTIFICATION
Leaves are needles up to 15cm long, carried in pairs on shoot. Bark is very dark brown and wrinkled with age. The needles, and indeed the whole tree, appear very dark in colour, and with Austrian Pine's bulkier, denser habit are an aid to distinguishing this subspecies from relatives such as the Corsican Pine (ssp. *laricio*) and Crimean Pine (ssp. *pallasiana*).

STATUS AND COMMENTS
Austrian Pine originates in S Austria, Italy and the Balkans; its relatives (see above) are similarly linked by their names to their homelands. Corsican Pine is quite common in Britain.

SPOTTER'S CHART

LOCATION	DATE/TIME

KEY FACT   This tree does well on calcareous soils and also by the sea, where it is often planted to provide shelter and stabilise sand-dunes.

MARITIME PINE
Pinus pinaster

FACT FILE

SIZE Height to 35m HABITAT Most often found in seaside plantations in the S and W FLOWERS Apr–Jun HABIT Often with a spreading crown, and may be bent by the wind. Conifer

IDENTIFICATION
Leaves are very long needles, up to 25cm long, carried in pairs. Cones are brown, tend to stay on tree, and are notable for being shiny. Bark is dark purple-brown and may become very plated in mature trees. Older trees are often picturesquely windswept and devoid of lower branches.

STATUS AND COMMENTS
Maritime Pine's native habitats are on the Mediterranean coastline; in Britain it grows best by the sea, where it is nearly always planted rather then self-sowing.

KEY FACT

The sap from the Maritime Pine is an important source of natural turpentine. The tree is also known as **Cluster Pine**, because of its groups of cones.

SPOTTER'S CHART

LOCATION	DATE/TIME

FACT FILE **SIZE** Height to 30m **HABITAT** Shelter belts, parks and larger gardens **FLOWERS** May–Jun **HABIT** Young trees are tall and thin; old trees have a pronounced dome and dense look. Conifer

IDENTIFICATION

Leaves are long, thin needles held in threes on stem; very bright green. Cones are green when young, brown when old, and may stay on tree for years; notably asymmetrical. Bark is dark brown, greying and wrinkling with age. Older trees may have heavy, spreading limbs that touch the ground.

STATUS AND COMMENTS

In Britain, this native of **W** coastal **USA** is most likely to be found on light soils in the mild **S** and **W**, often by the sea.

> **KEY FACT**
>
> In its native range, this tree is now found in only a handful of sites around Monterey, California. The cones release their seeds only when heated by fire. Ironically, the tree grows much faster in Britain than in the USA.

SPOTTER'S CHART

LOCATION	DATE/TIME

WEYMOUTH PINE
Pinus strobus

FACT FILE

SIZE Height to 50m HABITAT Plantations; also some parks and gardens FLOWERS May–Jun HABIT Tall and straight, with horizontal branches holding plates of foliage. Conifer

IDENTIFICATION

Leaves are slim needles up to 15cm long, held in fives on shoot; blue-green. Cones are slim and less than 20cm long; green, ageing to brown. Bark is dark grey. Branches tend to be conspicuously horizontal, and carry dense plates of distinctive blue-green foliage.

KEY FACT

The tree's British common name comes from Captain George Weymouth, the 17th-century explorer who imported it to England from E North America, where it is known as the Eastern White Pine.

STATUS AND COMMENTS

This handsome and distinctive tree, a native of eastern North America, is not as widely seen in Britain as in other parts of Europe, where it is a popular and successful timber species.

SPOTTER'S CHART

LOCATION	DATE/TIME

FACT FILE SIZE Height to 25m HABITAT Riversides, canal-sides, damp woodlands FLOWERS Apr HABIT Mature trees often stumpy, with low branches from stout bole; spreading, domed crown. Deciduous

IDENTIFICATION
Leaves are up to 15cm long, hairless, coarse-toothed; blue-white on underside. Male (yellow) and female (green) catkins are borne on separate trees. Bark is dark brown with deep fissures. Roots are red in water (those of White Willow are white).

STATUS AND COMMENTS
A widespread native species. It is very often spread along watercourses from pieces that have broken off another tree upstream, creating a network of genetically identical trees.

KEY FACT
True to both its English and Latin names, this tree's branches and twigs do indeed break off and/or fall off with great ease. Mature trees on riverbanks and canal banks may be pollarded, or may have broken branches.

SPOTTER'S CHART

LOCATION	DATE/TIME

WHITE WILLOW
Salix alba

SIZE Height to 25m **HABITAT** Riversides, canal-sides, wet woods and meadows **FLOWERS** Apr–May **HABIT** Columnar, with ascending branches; mature trees have a dense crown. Deciduous

IDENTIFICATION
Leaves are up to 8cm long (shorter than those of Crack Willow), softly hairy on both sides and finely toothed. Bark is greyish brown with a network of fissures. In winter, roots in water are white (they are red in Crack Willow).

STATUS AND COMMENTS
The native White Willow is common everywhere, but can be mistaken for the very similar Cricket-Bat Willow (var. *caerulea*), which has reddish shoots and much more vigorous growth.

KEY FACT
White Willow is not nearly as prone to breaking branches and stems as Crack Willow. In a breeze it appears silvery green, whereas Crack Willow appears plain green at all times. It is quite often pollarded, especially beside watercourses.

SPOTTER'S CHART

LOCATION	DATE/TIME

GREY WILLOW (COMMON SALLOW)
Salix cinerea

FACT FILE   SIZE Height to 6m HABITAT Widespread, especially
in uncultivated wet or damp sites FLOWERS Mar–Apr
HABIT Usually a bushy shrub rather than a tree. Deciduous

IDENTIFICATION

Leaves are rounded rectangles, broader in the middle, and proportionally much longer than those of Goat Willow; dark green. Catkins, or pussies, are smaller than those of Goat Willow. Bark is greyish green with vertical fissures. Has notably thick grey twigs.

STATUS AND COMMENTS

The native Grey Willow, of which there are several subspecies, is common throughout Britain. It is less likely to be seen on drier soils than Goat Willow.

SPOTTER'S CHART

LOCATION	DATE/TIME

KEY FACT   Grey Willow and Goat Willow are very similar and, confusingly, are both often called Common Sallow. Grey Willow flowers later than Goat Willow and has smaller catkins.

PURPLE WILLOW
Salix purpurea

FACT FILE

SIZE Height to 6m HABITAT Wet places: beside rivers and ponds, and in marshes FLOWERS Mar–Apr HABIT Most often seen as a stocky shrub, but sometimes a small tree. Deciduous

IDENTIFICATION

Leaves are up to 12cm long, widening out towards tip; light green; often grow in pairs on opposite sides of shoot, with next pair at angle of 180°. Young shoots and other parts of tree are purplish. Bark is grey and notably shiny.

KEY FACT
Purple Willow is frequently found as a coppiced plant, its vigorous shoots being cut for basketry. It is sometimes called Purple Osier.

STATUS AND COMMENTS

A locally common native in Britain, this species is most likely to be found in C and N England. It was once widely planted in the areas where it does occur. Rare or absent elsewhere.

SPOTTER'S CHART

LOCATION	DATE/TIME

FACT FILE

SIZE **Height to 3m** HABITAT **Wet, acidic soils, typically in the N and W** FLOWERS **Mar–Apr** HABIT **Low, spreading bush – a shrub rather than a tree. Deciduous**

IDENTIFICATION

Leaves are up to 4cm long, broader at tip. 'Ears' (properly called stipules) on leaf stem directly below leaf but separate from it are a key clue to identification. Male plant has yellow catkins in spring. Bark is grey and smooth. Low-growing.

STATUS AND COMMENTS

This unassuming native plant is widespread in wetter **W** and **N** areas, and is especially typical of Scottish forests, wet hillsides and stream-sides. It grows as far **N** as the Shetlands.

KEY FACT

Eared Willow is a 'pioneer' plant, being one of the first to colonise bare or recently cleared ground. Like all willows, it is also an important foodplant for moths and other insects.

SPOTTER'S CHART

LOCATION	DATE/TIME

WEEPING WILLOW
Salix × sepulcralis **'Chrysocoma'**

SIZE Height to 20m HABITAT Parks, gardens, watersides FLOWERS Mar–Apr HABIT Archetypal 'weeping' outline on an elegant trunk. Highly distinctive. Deciduous

IDENTIFICATION
Leaves are up to 12cm long, thin, with a tapering point; carried on delicate, slender shoots; bright green above, blue-green below. Bark is pale browny grey. The weeping outline is provided by the many long, hanging shoots, which may extend down to the ground.

KEY FACT
This is a 'man-made' tree – a hybrid of White Willow and Chinese Weeping Willow. As with all hybrids, it is very vigorous and not at all suitable for small gardens, although it is often seen in them!

STATUS AND COMMENTS
Familiar in municipal parks and gardens, and alongside rivers and canals, for many the hybrid Weeping Willow is the quintessential tree of hot, lazy summer days.

SPOTTER'S CHART

LOCATION	DATE/TIME

FACT FILE

SIZE Height to 8m **HABITAT** Watersides and, traditionally, withy beds **FLOWERS** Mar–Apr **HABIT** Rarely, if ever, seen as a 'maiden' tree; either a pollard or a coppice. Deciduous

KEY FACT

When basket-making was an essential industry, withy beds were widespread (withies are the flexible young stems), especially in Somerset and East Anglia, and in marshy areas. Today, there are far fewer commercial beds.

IDENTIFICATION

Leaves are up to 15cm long, thin; dark green above, much lighter below. Bark on pollards (many stems arising from a bole) is often grey. Pollards are usually found on watersides, and coppices (many stems growing from a stub) in marshes and wet places.

STATUS AND COMMENTS

There are at least 60 cultivars of Common Osier, selected for their different colours and pliability, including 'Black Maul', 'Flanders Red' and 'Holton's Black'.

SPOTTER'S CHART

LOCATION	DATE/TIME

GOAT WILLOW (PUSSY WILLOW)
Salix caprea

SIZE Height to 15m **HABITAT** Woods, hedgerows, **FACT FILE**
waste places **FLOWERS** Feb–Apr **HABIT** In the open can be bushy
and rounded; tall and straggly if overshadowed. Deciduous

KEY FACT

Goat Willow is one of our most important trees for wildlife, being the foodplant for the larvae of many insects, moths and butterflies. In spring, the catkins provide essential early food for bees and other insects. It is often confused with Grey Willow, but it flowers earlier and has larger catkins.

IDENTIFICATION

Leaves are oval with a bent tip; darkening with age from bright to dull green, undersides grey-green. Male catkins are bright yellow and very conspicuous on bare trees; female catkins are greener and produce dense drifts of wispy white seeds. Bark is grey, becoming ridged with age.

SPOTTER'S CHART

LOCATION	DATE/TIME

STATUS AND COMMENTS

The native Goat Willow is very common and widespread in Britain, tolerating drier soils than most other willows. It is a modest tree, often overlooked once flowering is over.

FACT FILE SIZE Height to 35m in Britain HABITAT Occasional; most often seen as a specimen tree FLOWERS Apr–May HABIT Tall and thin with a narrow conical crown. Deciduous

IDENTIFICATION

Leaves are up to 25cm long, elongated arrowhead in shape; glossy green above, very pale (almost white) underneath, yellow in autumn. Bark is silvery brown, becoming ridged with age. Whole plant is sweetly scented, especially in spring.

STATUS AND COMMENTS

A native of W North America, this tree is uncommon in Britain, where it is prone to early death, often as a result of canker. It grows very tall very fast.

SPOTTER'S CHART

LOCATION	DATE/TIME

KEY FACT In its native habitat the Western Balsam Poplar can grow to a mighty 70m. It is sometimes grown for its resin and hybridises easily with the very similar Balsam Poplar.

WHITE POPLAR
Populus alba

SIZE **Height to 30m** HABITAT **Parks, gardens, municipal planting, shelter belts** FLOWERS **Mar–Apr** HABIT **Classic 'tree shape', but often lopsided, and suckers at base. Deciduous**

IDENTIFICATION
Leaves are variable: on strong shoots they are deeply lobed and maple-like; on lesser shoots they are still lobed but much more rounded; all are dark green above, bright white and thickly hairy below. Male catkins are grey with crimson stamens; female catkins are green. Bark is white to grey.

STATUS AND COMMENTS
Probably not native to our region, this commonly planted tree is popular for its striking white appearance when the undersides of the leaves are upturned in the wind. It is often seen by the sea, and is salt-tolerant.

KEY FACT

This tree was probably introduced to Britain, but grows widely throughout Europe, parts of Asia and North Africa. It may form thickets by suckering.

SPOTTER'S CHART

LOCATION	DATE/TIME

FACT FILE   SIZE Height to 35m HABITAT Widespread, but does best on calcareous soils FLOWERS Feb HABIT Large-limbed, impressive tree with a dominant trunk. Deciduous

IDENTIFICATION

Leaves are oval or heart-shaped with rounded teeth, but variable; dark green above, lighter and densely hairy below. Male catkins are white with red stamens; female catkins are green. Bark is white to grey, with diamond-shaped fissures on older trees. Can form thickets by suckering.

KEY FACT   Grey Poplar is a hybrid of White Poplar and Aspen, and is described by botanists as 'stable' – meaning that it cross-breeds true to create Grey Poplar again and again.

SPOTTER'S CHART

LOCATION	DATE/TIME

STATUS AND COMMENTS

Though widespread, Grey Poplar is more likely to be seen near watercourses in areas of chalk or limestone. In such places its massive shape frequently causes it to stand out.

ASPEN
Populus tremula

FACT FILE

SIZE Height to 20m HABITAT Widespread, thriving on damp, poor soils FLOWERS Feb–Mar HABIT Lightly branched and often spindly with a light crown. Deciduous

KEY FACT
Aspen leaves rustle and move even when there seems to be little or no breeze. They flutter more than any other poplar, making this a sure way of discovering this tree in the landscape.

STATUS AND COMMENTS
Aspen is a common but unobtrusive and frequently overlooked native. It suckers freely and often forms small groves.

IDENTIFICATION
Leaves are oval and toothed; darker green above than below. Catkins are reddish and drooping; males are darker than females. Produces large quantities of tiny white seeds. Bark is grey and smooth in young trees, becoming darker and pitted with age.

SPOTTER'S CHART

LOCATION	DATE/TIME

FACT FILE
SIZE Height to 28m HABITAT 'Wild' trees are often associated with damp places; also planted in cities
FLOWERS Mar–Apr HABIT Imposing when mature. Deciduous

IDENTIFICATION

Leaves are shiny green, and triangular with rounded edges and fine teeth; they are rather like birch leaves, as the subspecies' name suggests. Catkins are slightly drooping and hard-looking. Bark is very dark brown in mature trees, often with burrs, snags and fissures. A burly, charismatic tree.

STATUS AND COMMENTS

This subspecies is considered native to Britain. There are probably only about 6,000 throughout the country, and the majority – if not all – of these are thought to have been planted.

> **KEY FACT**
>
> 'Manchester Poplar' is a male clone, planted in cities because it is resistant to pollution. The much rarer female produces vast amounts of fine, floaty white seed capsules – not popular in cities!

SPOTTER'S CHART

LOCATION	DATE/TIME

LOMBARDY POPLAR
Populus nigra 'Italica'

FACT FILE

SIZE Height to 36m HABITAT Parks, roadsides, avenues FLOWERS Apr–May HABIT Tall, thin columnar tree; variants have slightly differing appearances. Deciduous

IDENTIFICATION
Leaves are small and broadly triangular in shape, with long points. Catkins on male trees are bright red. Bark is greyish brown, with a gnarly appearance in older trees. There are several named varieties, which, though not especially common, are planted throughout Britain.

KEY FACT
The 'typical' Lombardy Poplar is a tall, thin male tree (female trees are rare). On its introduction to Britain it was immediately popular for its architectural impact on the landscape.

STATUS AND COMMENTS
The Lombardy Poplar originates in the Po Valley in Italy and was introduced first to France and then Britain in the mid-18th century. In Britain it is frequently planted in 'avenues', like those so often seen lining roads in France.

SPOTTER'S CHART

LOCATION	DATE/TIME

HYBRID BLACK POPLAR
Populus × canadensis

FACT FILE SIZE Height to 30m HABITAT Parks, gardens, plantations, amenity planting FLOWERS Mar–Apr HABIT Imposing and densely leaved; variable, as there are several cultivars. Deciduous

IDENTIFICATION
Leaves are shiny green, rounded triangular in shape and finely toothed. Male trees have bright red catkins in spring. Clouds of white seeds are released in midsummer from female trees (Black Poplar releases seeds much earlier). Bark is dark grey, often with fissures.

KEY FACT
The tree is a hybrid between the European Black Poplar and the North American Cottonwood. Its various cultivars, including trees with yellow, coppery or golden leaves, are all known for their hybrid vigour.

SPOTTER'S CHART

LOCATION	DATE/TIME

STATUS AND COMMENTS
This is a much more common tree than the Black Poplar, but the wide range of cultivars can make identification tricky. It prefers drier, warmer sites than the Black Poplar.

COMMON WALNUT
Juglans regia

SIZE Height to 30m **HABITAT** Parks, large gardens, hedgerows, orchards **FLOWERS** Late Apr–late May
HABIT Handsome, full domed and robust when mature. Deciduous

KEY FACT

Common Walnut wood is still highly prized and sought after by cabinetmakers. The 'burr-wood' unique to the species is especially valuable for veneers and fetches very high prices. The tree's distinctive heady scent (try rubbing the leaves) is not liked by all.

IDENTIFICATION

Leaves are dark green and waxy-looking, in pairs of leaflets on long twigs with one leaflet at tip. Catkins in spring are prone to frosts. Fruits are green, enclosing a brown nut. Bark is silvery grey.

STATUS AND COMMENTS

Introduced to Britain by the Romans, the Common Walnut is now widespread here, although single trees often go unnoticed in the countryside. It has been grown for centuries for its nuts, which some prefer to eat 'green' rather than mature and 'brown'. Birds such as crows like them too!

SPOTTER'S CHART

LOCATION	DATE/TIME

FACT FILE SIZE Height to 30m HABITAT Woodland, heathland, moors, parks, gardens FLOWERS Feb–Apr HABIT Straight and graceful when young; drooping branches when mature. Deciduous

IDENTIFICATION
Leaves are small, light, rounded triangles, with small, ragged teeth; green, turning golden yellow in autumn. Male and female catkins – appearing first in winter – are carried on same tree. Bark develops from smooth silvery white in young trees to deep, dark fissures low on the trunk on mature trees.

STATUS AND COMMENTS
A very widespread native throughout Britain, from mountains to heaths, and from the wildest landscapes to suburban gardens. Much loved for its delicate looks and white papery bark.

KEY FACT
Silver Birch is excellent for wildlife: some fungi depend on it; lichens and mosses grow on it; birds such as tits seek out food in its leaves and fissured bark. It casts light, dappled shade, making it an ideal garden tree.

SPOTTER'S CHART

LOCATION	DATE/TIME

DOWNY BIRCH
Betula pubescens

FACT FILE

SIZE Height to 28m HABITAT Common, especially on poor, peaty soils – moors, heaths and uplands FLOWERS Apr–May HABIT Modest and upright, often with an untidy crown. Deciduous

IDENTIFICATION
Leaves are very similar to those of Silver Birch, but rounder and with more uniform teeth. Bark is reddish, becoming greyish brown with age; never has the deeply fissured appearance of Silver Birch's lower trunk. Twigs are hairy. Branches are upright, not drooping – another difference from Silver Birch.

KEY FACT
Downy Birch is one of those plants that foresters sometimes call 'weeds' – a tree that grows very fast on recently cleared or burnt ground and can become invasive. Its common name comes from the hairy twigs.

STATUS AND COMMENTS
The native Downy Birch sometimes grows next to the Silver Birch, but the former is more commonly seen in the N and W, and in wilder, less cultivated places.

SPOTTER'S CHART

LOCATION	DATE/TIME

PAPER-BARK BIRCH (CANOE BIRCH)
Betula papyrifera

SIZE Height to 25m HABITAT Parks, gardens, hedges, amenity planting FLOWERS Feb–Apr HABIT Broadly conical tree, often more stout than the Silver Birch. Deciduous

IDENTIFICATION
Leaves are larger than those of most other birches (up to 10cm long and 7.5cm across); toothed, with a tapering point, and carried on hairy stalks; dark green above, lighter below, turning yellow and then orange in autumn. Bark is white-orange.

STATUS AND COMMENTS
A native of North America, where it is widespread and common, this attractive tree is used in planting schemes and in gardens across Britain, although it is not that common here.

KEY FACT
The papery outer bark peels easily to reveal pink, browns and whites beneath. The bark was used by Native Americans to build their canoes – hence the tree's alternative common name of Canoe Birch.

SPOTTER'S CHART

LOCATION	DATE/TIME

HIMALAYAN BIRCH
Betula utilis

FACT FILE

SIZE Height to 25m HABITAT Parks, gardens, amenity planting FLOWERS Mar–May HABIT Conical and rounded in mature, free-standing trees. Deciduous

IDENTIFICATION
Leaves are up to 10cm long and 6cm across; dark green, sometimes glossy above. Bark ranges from dark, shiny browns through pink to white; peels horizontally; rows of dark brown horizontal dotted lines ('lenticels') are often noticeable.

STATUS AND COMMENTS
Introduced to Britain in 1849, Himalayan Birch is a native of the Himalayas, where it is traditionally used to make paper, in buildings and, of course, as a fine firewood.

KEY FACT

Cultivated varieties of this birch are increasingly planted for their striking bark; in var. *jacquemontii*, for example, it is a gleaming white. The bark is sometimes even scrubbed to make it shine all the more.

SPOTTER'S CHART

LOCATION	DATE/TIME

FACT FILE
SIZE Height to 5m HABITAT Parks, some gardens
FLOWERS Mar–Apr HABIT At best a small tree in
Britain, but most often seen as a shrub. Deciduous

IDENTIFICATION

Leaves are up to 6cm long,
with sharp teeth and a
pointed tip; dark green above,
lighter beneath. Male catkins
are yellow, females green; ripe
brown fruits often stay on
tree throughout winter. Bark
is brown.

STATUS AND COMMENTS

This native of mountainous
regions of central and E Europe
is not a common tree in Britain;
it is most likely to be encountered
as an ornamental specimen in
arboretums and some parks
and gardens.

KEY FACT

In its native habitat
the Green Alder can regenerate from
its roots after being flattened by
avalanches. Its clumps of stems can
make it look rather like Hazel.

SPOTTER'S CHART

LOCATION	DATE/TIME

ITALIAN ALDER
Alnus cordata

FACT FILE

SIZE **Height to 26m** HABITAT **Parks, gardens, arboretums, roadsides** FLOWERS **Feb–Mar** HABIT **Tall, handsome tree when mature, broadly conical in outline. Deciduous**

KEY FACT Introduced to Britain in 1820, this tree is considered by many experts to be the most handsome and noble of all the alders.

STATUS AND COMMENTS
Italian Alder (native to S Italy and Corsica) grows in a wide variety of conditions in Britain, even on dry chalk, but does best where there is moisture in the soil.

IDENTIFICATION
Leaves are heart-shaped and finely toothed; glossy dark green above, undersides with orange hairs along midrib. Yellow male catkins and notably large, ripe brown catkin fruits are prominent. Bark is pale grey and smooth, becoming fissured with age.

SPOTTER'S CHART

LOCATION	DATE/TIME

FACT FILE

SIZE **Height to 25m** HABITAT **River- and stream-sides, bogs, carrs** FLOWERS **Feb–Mar** HABIT **Can be tall and rather conical; more often slightly twisty; also coppiced. Deciduous**

IDENTIFICATION

Leaves are rounded, with slightly wavy edges culminating in an apex that is either flat or slightly indented; glossy, dark green. Female flowers develop first into green, then ripe brown 'cones' that often noticeably adorn the tree in winter. Bark is brown, becoming fissured with age.

KEY FACT

As well as being important in stabilising banks, Common Alder was once a significant commercial crop – clogs were one of the items made from its wood. It is a superb tree for wildlife, especially insects and birds.

STATUS AND COMMENTS

A widely distributed native tree that suffered in the 20th century as a result of the discredited fashion for straightening and 'tidying' rivers and streams. More recently it has suffered further from a waterborne disease.

SPOTTER'S CHART

LOCATION	DATE/TIME

HAZEL
Corylus avellana

FACT FILE

SIZE Height to 15m **HABITAT** Woods and hedgerows; also Hazel copses **FLOWERS** Late Jan–Mar **HABIT** By nature a large, multi-stemmed shrub; often coppiced. Deciduous

IDENTIFICATION

Leaves are rounded, with a point at apex, and toothed; dark green, rough and hairy. Infant catkins appear in late autumn; by early spring, yellow male catkins are prominent. Female flowers are minute and red. Fruit is a brown nut, partly encased in a papery shuck; edible. Bark is a burnished brown colour.

STATUS AND COMMENTS

A very widespread and common native. The practical uses of its wood are unparalleled – hurdles, thatching spars, clothes pegs, walking sticks, firewood, etc. – and once employed tens of thousands of woodland craftsmen.

KEY FACT

Traditionally managed Hazel copses are habitat for some of Britain's rarest and most beautiful butterflies and a myriad other insects, as well as being superb for wildflowers and grasses. Very old, outgrown coppice stems can be mistaken for a Hazel 'tree'.

SPOTTER'S CHART

LOCATION	DATE/TIME

FACT FILE SIZE Height to 15m HABITAT Gardens, orchards and wider countryside FLOWERS Feb–Mar HABIT Almost identical to Hazel, but grown for its nuts rather than its wood. Deciduous

IDENTIFICATION

Leaves are very similar to those of Hazel; perhaps more serrated. Bark is a burnished brown colour. The nuts make it most distinct from Hazel: significantly larger and longer comparatively than the rounded Hazel nut, and enclosed in a bigger, tight-fitting shuck, the 'involucre'.

KEY FACT Filberts have been grown commercially for their nuts over a huge area. In Britain, the 'Kentish Cob' cultivar might be a hybrid with Hazel.

STATUS AND COMMENTS

A native of the Balkans, this tree is as likely to be seen these days as the purple garden cultivar 'Purpurea', which has markedly more fragile stems and twigs than the true species.

SPOTTER'S CHART

LOCATION	DATE/TIME

HORNBEAM
Carpinus betulus

SIZE Height to 30m **HABITAT** Woods, forests, copses, hedges **FLOWERS** Apr–May **HABIT** Mature tree is stocky and elegant, with plentiful upturning branches. Deciduous

IDENTIFICATION
Leaves are up to 12cm long; oval, with a very pointed end and double-toothed; dark green, with very noticeable veins and hairy undersides. Catkins are long and drooping. Fruit begins green, turning yellow-gold; enclosed in dangling, three-lobed bracts – quite unlike those of Common Beech. Bark is grey, becoming distinctly fluted with age.

KEY FACT
Hornbeam was once much prized for its wood, which is very hardwearing and was used for such things as cogs, chopping blocks and wheel parts. The tree was also coppiced for tough, long-lasting poles.

STATUS AND COMMENTS
Hornbeam is a common British native that is frequently mistaken for Common Beech. Both are widely used for hedging and both retain their leaves long into winter.

SPOTTER'S CHART

LOCATION	DATE/TIME

FACT FILE   SIZE Height to 40m HABITAT Woods, forests, parks, gardens, hedges FLOWERS Apr–May HABIT Mature trees very large and elegant, with long branches. Frequently used in hedging. Deciduous

KEY FACT
Mature Common Beech trees cast such a dense shade that few plants can live beneath them, and Common Beech hedges frequently retain their leaves all winter. Beech-mast (the fruit) was once a staple winter diet of foraging pigs.

STATUS AND COMMENTS
Possibly native to S Britain, the species is common and widespread but is very much associated with downland landscapes, where Beech 'hangers' are characteristic.

IDENTIFICATION
Leaves are up to 10cm long; oval, pointed at the end and with wavy edges; bright, light green in spring, becoming dark and then often bronze or golden in autumn. Flowers are dangling, furry and blob-like. Fruits are shiny brown nuts in a wiry case. Bark is grey.

SPOTTER'S CHART

LOCATION	DATE/TIME

SWEET CHESTNUT
Castanea sativa

FACT FILE

SIZE Height to 36m HABITAT Woods, parks, large gardens FLOWERS May–Jun HABIT Most often noticed as a large, dominant, leafy tree with obvious twisting bark on bole. Deciduous

IDENTIFICATION

Leaves are very large and long, with spiny teeth along whole length; deep, shiny green, often turning browny gold in autumn. Flowers are dense bunches of highly scented yellow catkins. Fruit is a glossy brown nut encased in very spiny husk. Bark is silvery grey.

STATUS AND COMMENTS

Introduced to Britain by the Romans, this native of Continental Europe and North Africa is more often associated with sandy and acid soils, and is not nearly so common on chalky or limey soils.

KEY FACT

A common tree, still widely planted for its poles and wood. The edible nuts crop well only in favourable years; most often the nuts on British trees are much smaller than those from European trees selected for their fruits.

SPOTTER'S CHART

LOCATION	DATE/TIME

ENGLISH OAK (PEDUNCULATE OAK)

Quercus robur

SIZE **Height to 40m** HABITAT **Woods, hedgerows, open countryside, parks, large gardens** FLOWERS **Apr–May** HABIT **Majestic when mature: large and heavy-branched. Deciduous**

KEY FACT English Oak is extremely important for wildlife: it can teem with insects, the entire tree seeming alive with these creatures, which in turn attract birds that feed their young on caterpillars.

IDENTIFICATION

Leaves are deeply and irregularly lobed, with prominent veins; bright green when young, becoming dark and leathery; joined to twig by a very short stalk. Flowers are dangling yellow strings. Fruit, an acorn, is held in a cup on a long stalk. Bark is grey, becoming deeply fissured and wrinkled with age.

STATUS AND COMMENTS

The native English Oak grows on most soil types, but has a preference for clay. It is still a very important timber crop. Very old trees – often pollards – might be 800 or 900 years old.

SPOTTER'S CHART

LOCATION	DATE/TIME

SESSILE OAK (DURMAST OAK)
Quercus petraea

FACT FILE

SIZE Height to 42m HABITAT Woods, open countryside, parks, larger gardens FLOWERS May HABIT Mature trees tall and gracious; less 'branchy' than English Oak. Deciduous

IDENTIFICATION
Leaves are deeply lobed and held on twig by a long stalk; dark green. Flowers are drooping and greenish. Acorn cup attaches directly to twig without a stalk. Bark is grey, becoming fissured with age. Often has a longer trunk than English Oak, and a lighter canopy.

KEY FACT
Sessile Oak was once an important commercial tree; today, it is hugely important for wildlife. Old, outgrown coppices on uplands and wilder riversides are especially rich habitats for dependent species, and often have attractive ground flora.

STATUS AND COMMENTS
A widespread native and the most common oak in some areas, especially on lighter soils and in the W, Wales and the N.

SPOTTER'S CHART

LOCATION	DATE/TIME

HUNGARIAN OAK
Quercus frainetto

FACT FILE   SIZE **Height to 38m** HABITAT **Parks, large gardens** FLOWERS **May–Jun** HABIT **When mature, is a distinctive, gracious oak, with a rounded, symmetrical outline. Deciduous**

IDENTIFICATION
Leaves are large (up to 25cm long) and distinctive, with very deep neatly cut lobes; dark green. Flower spikes are smallish and dangling. Fruit is an egg-shaped acorn held in a downy cup. Bark is mid-grey; mature trees may have tidy fissures and plates on lower trunk. Branches are straight.

STATUS AND COMMENTS
A native of Hungary, central Europe and S Italy, this is a tree that in Britain you are more likely to see in a park or tree collection than in the wider countryside.

KEY FACT
Hungarian Oak is liked for its elegant, distinguished looks. It can hybridise with other oaks, including English Oak, on which it is also sometimes grafted.

SPOTTER'S CHART

LOCATION	DATE/TIME

CORK OAK
Quercus suber

FACT FILE

SIZE **Height to 20m** HABITAT **In Britain, parks, arboretums and large gardens** FLOWERS **May** HABIT **Mature trees are impressive, with a domed, spreading appearance. Evergreen**

IDENTIFICATION

Leaves are up to 7cm long; glossy, dark green above, paler below and finely hairy. Acorns are held in scaly cups. Bark is highly distinctive: grey; in older trees it becomes very thick, and deeply fissured and ridged – it feels like cork because it is cork!

KEY FACT
The advent of plastic wine-bottle stoppers has threatened the Mediterranean Cork Oak plantations and forests, endangering a unique and rich wildlife habitat. In parts of Portugal, Cork Oak forests are now being conserved.

STATUS AND COMMENTS

Grown in Britain as an ornamental tree. In its Mediterranean home, the tree was (and still is) stripped of some of its bark every seven or so years, suffering no harm in the process.

SPOTTER'S CHART

LOCATION	DATE/TIME

FACT FILE SIZE Height to 38m HABITAT Parks, arboretums, large gardens, and in the countryside FLOWERS May–Jun HABIT Mature trees are very spreading and domed. Deciduous

IDENTIFICATION

Leaves are long (up to 12cm) and thin; often with very deep lobes, usually rounded at tip; dark green and leathery above, lighter and downy beneath. Acorn is carried in a cup with whiskery scales. Bark is grey-brown and thick, becoming deeply fissured and ridged.

KEY FACT

Though admired as a handsome ornament, the Turkey Oak has no value as a timber tree. It is host to a gall wasp that attacks the acorns of English Oak with destructive effect.

STATUS AND COMMENTS

The Turkey Oak was introduced to Britain in 1735, and has since been widely planted; it now seeds itself freely. It grows fast, even on poor, thin soils.

SPOTTER'S CHART

LOCATION	DATE/TIME

HOLM OAK
Quercus ilex

SIZE **Height to 30m** HABITAT **Hedgerows, shelter belts, parks, gardens** FLOWERS **Jun** HABIT **Broad and domed, with straight branches and a dense appearance. Evergreen**

IDENTIFICATION
Leaves are wavy and evergreen; very dark green above and leathery, grey and felty underneath; some have spines. Flowers are bright golden in early summer. Acorns sit in a felty cup. Bark is very dark (almost black) and sometimes appears dusty.

SPOTTER'S CHART

LOCATION	DATE/TIME

STATUS AND COMMENTS
The Holm Oak is a native of **S Europe** and has been widely planted in **Britain** since it was introduced in the **16th century**. It is often used as evergreen hedging and as shelter belts for other trees, and as it is very tolerant of salt spray it is also often grown by the sea.

KEY FACT
This species sheds its leaves in summer, when many think it at its most attractive, with new shoots and catkins on display.

SIZE Height to 35m HABITAT Parks, gardens; sometimes in commercial plantations FLOWERS May HABIT Mature trees are domed and spreading, with sturdy branches. Deciduous

IDENTIFICATION

Leaves are big, often up to 22cm long and 15cm wide at widest point; have deep lobes ending with whiskery teeth; matt green above, paler beneath.

KEY FACT Red Oak has often been planted for its bright (sometimes spectacular) autumn colours. It can be mistaken for the similar-looking Scarlet Oak, and the Pin and Shumard oaks.

Acorns take two years to ripen. Bark is silvery grey, sometimes becoming scaly with age.

STATUS AND COMMENTS

Red Oak is fairly commonly encountered in Britain, nearly always in cultivation. It is a native of E North America.

SPOTTER'S CHART

LOCATION	DATE/TIME

SCARLET OAK
Quercus coccinea

FACT FILE

SIZE Height to 30m HABITAT Parks, larger gardens, tree collections FLOWERS May–Jun HABIT Slender cone shape, with well-spaced, rather untidy branches. Deciduous

IDENTIFICATION
Leaves are up to 10cm long; very deeply cut lobes, middle lobe longest, with whiskery teeth at ends; glossy on both sides. Acorn ripens in second year; half of it is held in a cup (in Red Oak, only a quarter of acorn is held in cup). Bark is greyish brown; smooth, becoming ridged.

STATUS AND COMMENTS
Scarlet Oak was introduced to Britain from E North America and is grown here for its potentially spectacular autumn colours. The cultivar 'Splendens' is considered especially fine. It prefers warmer climates.

KEY FACT

This tree is quite easily confused with its American relatives, including Red Oak, as well as Pin and Shumard oaks, all of which are also grown for their beautiful autumn colours.

SPOTTER'S CHART

LOCATION	DATE/TIME

FACT FILE

SIZE **Height to 40m** HABITAT **Hedges, fields, open countryside; prefers to be near water** FLOWERS **Feb–Mar** HABIT **Huge and shapely when mature; willowy when young. Deciduous**

IDENTIFICATION

Leaves are large, up to 18cm long; oval or round, with a tapering point at tip; asymmetrical at base, where long side touches twig; dark green and rough. Bark is browny grey, becoming rough with age. Does not produce suckers.

KEY FACT

This is the only elm that is indisputably native to Britain (even English Elm has an uncertain history) – Wych Elm is found in so many places, including very remote spots, that experts accept its native ancestry.

STATUS AND COMMENTS

These days, as a result of Dutch Elm Disease, mature and semi-mature specimens of this native tree are uncommon in the S. The species is more likely to be encountered in the N and in Scotland.

SPOTTER'S CHART

LOCATION	DATE/TIME

ENGLISH ELM
Ulmus procera (syn. U. minor)

FACT FILE

SIZE Height to 36m **HABITAT** Woods, hedges, open country **FLOWERS** Feb–Mar **HABIT** Mature trees (now hardly ever seen) are enormous, asymmetrical and heavily branched. Deciduous

IDENTIFICATION
Leaves are up to 10cm long, hairy and uneven, oval or rounded; asymmetrical at base, with longest side not reaching to twig; point is not as tapering as in Wych Elm leaves. Bark is dark brown. Suckers have a spindly appearance and often occur in stands.

KEY FACT
English Elm suckers freely (unlike Wych Elm, which does not sucker), and this was its undoing, enabling Dutch Elm Disease to spread like wildfire through the genetically identical trees.

STATUS AND COMMENTS
English Elm was once one of our most iconic trees, and a common and much-loved giant. Dutch Elm Disease has, however, destroyed most – suckers grow to 6m or so and then succumb. Whether it is native or not is still a subject of research.

SPOTTER'S CHART

LOCATION	DATE/TIME

SMOOTH-LEAVED ELM
Ulmus minor (syn. U. carpinifolia)

FACT FILE SIZE Height to 30m HABITAT Restricted to some areas of S and E England FLOWERS Feb–Mar HABIT Mature trees are domed, spreading and sometimes pendulous. Deciduous

IDENTIFICATION

Leaves are up to 10cm long, smooth (hence species' common name), glossy and toothed; they are variable, often asymmetrical, the short side having a narrow taper. Bark is greyish brown, becoming scaly with ridges. Branches may be upright or drooping, depending on form.

KEY FACT

Smooth-leaved Elm is sometimes mistaken for Hornbeam. It has very close, and very similar, relatives in *Ulmus coritana* and *U. minor* f. *pendula*.

STATUS AND COMMENTS

In Britain, Smooth-leaved Elm occurs naturally only in a limited number of counties in the S and E, and may be further limited within those counties. It is widespread in Europe.

SPOTTER'S CHART

LOCATION	DATE/TIME

HUNTINGDON ELM
Ulmus × hollandica 'Vegeta'

FACT FILE

SIZE Height to 30m HABITAT Central England and East Anglia; also planted FLOWERS Feb–Mar HABIT Straight and domed, often with shoots and suckers at base. Deciduous

KEY FACT

Ulmus × hollandica is a naturally occurring hybrid found through much of Europe; the cultivar 'Vegeta', now known as the Huntingdon Elm, was raised in Huntingdonshire in the 18th century. Like other hybrid elms, Huntingdon Elm has some natural resistance to Dutch Elm Disease, so is still planted.

IDENTIFICATION

Leaves are up to 12cm long and toothed; dark and shiny on upperside; markedly asymmetrical, with short side tapering in at first vein. Bark is greyish brown, becoming regularly ridged with age. Branches are long, upright and lightly leaved.

STATUS AND COMMENTS

Though it is most often seen in central and E England, the hybrid Huntingdon Elm also occurs elsewhere as a planted tree on roadsides and in hedges.

SPOTTER'S CHART

LOCATION	DATE/TIME

COMMON MULBERRY (BLACK MULBERRY)
Morus nigra

FACT FILE SIZE Height to 12m HABITAT Parks and gardens
FLOWERS May HABIT Mature trees are picturesque, with a leaning
trunk topped by a mass of foliage. Deciduous

IDENTIFICATION
Leaves are up to 15cm long; heart-shaped, with a pointed tip; rough and glossy. Distinctive 'berry' fruits appear in midsummer, often in great profusion. Bark is dark orange-brown, and in mature trees often has many lumpy excrescences.

SPOTTER'S CHART

LOCATION	DATE/TIME

KEY FACT
The fruits are delicious, but only when fully ripe (nearly black). Children love them; parents possibly less so, since the juice dramatically stains both children and clothes.

STATUS AND COMMENTS
Common Mulberry has been planted in gardens and parks in Britain for centuries. The tree probably originally came from Asia, and it still prefers a warm spot in which to grow.

WHITE MULBERRY
Morus alba

SIZE Height to 15m HABITAT In warm areas as a cultivated tree FLOWERS May HABIT Mature trees are small and neat, with a polite dome. Deciduous

FACT FILE

IDENTIFICATION
Leaves are shiny and flimsy; variable in shape – oval to rounded, often with a heart-shaped base, sometimes lobed; smooth to the touch on upper surface, sometimes hairy underneath. 'Berry' fruits may be white, pink or darker red. Bark is grey, sometimes with a pink tinge.

KEY FACT
The fruits look similar to those of Black Mulberry, but are lighter in colour. Although edible in theory, they are tasteless in comparison, if not actually unpalatable.

SPOTTER'S CHART

LOCATION	DATE/TIME

STATUS AND COMMENTS
White Mulberry originates in China and was planted in Britain by silk workers in the 16th century, as the tree is the foodplant of silkworms. It is not common here, however, and is as likely to be found in a town garden as anywhere.

FACT FILE SIZE Height to 10m HABITAT Gardens, parks, waste ground FLOWERS May–Jul (flowers are invisible inside young fruit) HABIT Thickly leaved shrub. Deciduous

IDENTIFICATION

Leaves are large (up to 30cm long and wide), dark green, leathery and rough, with three to five very deep lobes and pronounced ribs and veins. Fruit may eventually ripen to brown or purple. Bark is dark grey and smooth. Trees in cultivation may be trained against a wall.

SPOTTER'S CHART

LOCATION	DATE/TIME

STATUS AND COMMENTS

This Asian native has long been cultivated in Britain for its fruits. It is also often found in such places as canal-sides, building plots and unkempt railway sidings.

KEY FACT

The flowers develop inside the young fruit, which has a small opening through which the flowers are reached by tiny wasps. Most figs in Britain can fruit without pollination, but will ripen only in warm, sheltered places.

BARBERRY
Berberis vulgaris

SIZE **Height to 4m** HABITAT **Hedgerows and** **FACT FILE**
waysides FLOWERS **Apr–May** HABIT **Almost never seen
as a stand-alone shrub; nearly always in a hedge. Deciduous**

IDENTIFICATION
Leaves are oval, dark green and toothed, with three sharp spines where leaf tufts meet shoot. Flowers are bright yellow, borne in prominent, drooping clusters. Fruit is a dark red oval. Bark is grey. Branches may be reddish. Does not look like anything else in the hedge.

KEY FACT
Barberry can be the host of a rust disease that can seriously damage wheat. For that reason it has been removed in the past, contributing to its scarcity in the countryside.

STATUS AND COMMENTS
Barberry is an uncommon and unevenly distributed British native, most likely to be found on chalky soils in the S. Its unusual leaves make it stand out in a hedge.

SPOTTER'S CHART

LOCATION	DATE/TIME

FACT FILE

SIZE **Height to 50m** HABITAT **Parks, gardens, arboretums** FLOWERS **Jun–Jul** HABIT **Majestic when mature, with huge lower branches; broadly columnar when young. Deciduous**

KEY FACT

Sometimes you can't see the 'tulips' very well high up on a mature Tulip Tree, but in any case the tree makes its best impact from its splendid profile and large, uniquely shaped leaves.

IDENTIFICATION

Leaves are very distinct: up to 20cm long and nearly as wide, with four large lobes, flat or indented at apex; bright, shiny green above, often golden in autumn. Flowers resemble greeny-yellow tulips. Bark is grey, becoming ridged with age.

STATUS AND COMMENTS

A native of North America, the Tulip Tree is widely planted in Britain. The best and most handsome specimens are nearly all in parks, large gardens and tree collections.

SPOTTER'S CHART

LOCATION	DATE/TIME

EVERGREEN MAGNOLIA
Magnolia grandiflora

SIZE Height to 25m HABITAT Parks, gardens, tree collections FLOWERS Jun–Nov HABIT Stand-alone trees are tall and spreading; often trained against a wall. Evergreen

IDENTIFICATION
Leaves are up to 20cm long and elliptical; dark green and glossy above, rust-coloured and woolly beneath. Flowers are creamy white, very large and scented; they start out conical but open out to as much as 25cm across. Bark is grey.

KEY FACT
The flowers do not all open at once, giving the tree a very long flowering period. There are many cultivated magnolias, including varieties of Evergreen Magnolia; some of these have flowers whose scent is almost overpowering at close range.

STATUS AND COMMENTS
Originally from the S USA, Evergreen Magnolia (also known as Bull Boy) has been planted in British gardens since the 18th century. It does best in warm, sheltered spots.

SPOTTER'S CHART

LOCATION	DATE/TIME

SWEET BAY (BAY)
Laurus nobilis

FACT FILE SIZE Height to 20m HABITAT Gardens, parks;
hardly ever seen outside of cultivation FLOWERS Jun
HABIT Bushy tree or shrub; often seen clipped to shape. Evergreen

IDENTIFICATION
Leaves are up to 10cm long; shiny, dark green above, paler beneath; leathery,
prominently veined and wavy-edged; give off a distinctive astringent,
peppery aroma when rubbed. Flowers are creamy white, borne in a cluster.
Fruit is a small green blob, ripening
to black. Bark is grey.

STATUS AND COMMENTS
Very widely planted for culinary
use and as a handsome shrub that
can be clipped into a variety of
shapes. The Sweet Bay can give
structure and formality to even
the smallest garden.

KEY FACT
As well as
cooking with it in much the
same ways we do today, the
Romans used Sweet Bay to
make garlands for poets,
athletes and nobles, including
emperors – hence the *nobilis*
part of the scientific name.

SPOTTER'S CHART

LOCATION	DATE/TIME

CALIFORNIAN LAUREL
Umbellularia californica

FACT FILE

SIZE Height to 20m HABITAT Some parks and
gardens FLOWERS Feb–Mar HABIT Similar to
Sweet Bay, but taller and more domed. Evergreen

IDENTIFICATION
Leaves are up to 9cm long (narrower than those of Sweet Bay), flat, and
bright green on both sides. Flowers are yellowish, borne in clusters. Fruit
begins as a small green berry, darkening to purple. Bark is dark grey.
Whole tree is unpleasantly odorous.

STATUS AND COMMENTS
A native of the USA; not a
commonly encountered tree in
Britain, where it is confined to
some parks, gardens and botanical
collections. It is similar to Sweet
Bay and can be mistaken for it.

KEY FACT

Just smelling
the Californian Laurel is enough
to give some people headaches,
bring on nausea, and even make
them pass out – hence it is often
called the Headache Tree. For
this reason it is best avoided.

SPOTTER'S CHART

LOCATION	DATE/TIME

SIZE Height to 30m **HABITAT** Parks, gardens, arboretums; favours deep, fertile soils **FLOWERS** May **HABIT** Large, handsome tree, conical but spreading. Deciduous

IDENTIFICATION
Leaves are up to 15cm long; palmately lobed, with five to seven deeply cut, finely toothed lobes, the terminal one longest; light green in summer, often turning intense yellows, purples and reds in autumn; have an aromatic scent when rubbed. Bark is greyish brown and ridged.

KEY FACT Sweet Gum (just as often known as Liquidambar) does not like shallow, dry soils, and is prone to frosts, especially when young. It is a tree that excites passion in tree-lovers.

STATUS AND COMMENTS
Sweet Gum is a native of SE USA and is widely planted in Britain, especially for its show of wonderful autumn colours. These are most reliable in the cultivar 'Lane Roberts'.

SPOTTER'S CHART

LOCATION	DATE/TIME

WITCH HAZEL (CHINESE WITCH HAZEL)
Hamamelis mollis

FACT FILE

SIZE Height to 5m **HABITAT** Parks, gardens, arboretums; prefers lime-free soils **FLOWERS** Jan–Mar
HABIT A tall Hazel-like shrub; not always elegant. Deciduous

KEY FACT
Witch Hazel is still regarded by many as the most handsome member of the *Hamamelis* genus and is very widely planted. Its petals are wider than those of many of its relatives.

IDENTIFICATION
Leaves are oval and toothed, similar to those of Hazel; dark green, turning lovely shades of yellow in autumn. Flower petals are wavy, spidery straps, always yellow in the true species; borne on branches long before leaves emerge; sweetly scented. Bark is greyish brown.

SPOTTER'S CHART

LOCATION	DATE/TIME

STATUS AND COMMENTS
There are several cultivated varieties of this native of China, raised for their flower colour and scent, and for leaf colour in the autumn; they are very often found in the winter gardens of larger gardens and arboretums.

JAPANESE WITCH HAZEL
Hamamelis japonica

FACT FILE SIZE Height to 15m HABITAT Parks, gardens, arboretums FLOWERS Jan–Mar HABIT Spreading, sometimes gangly, shrub. Superficially similar to Hazel. Deciduous

IDENTIFICATION
Leaves are oval and toothed, similar to those of Hazel; dark green, turning orange and red in autumn. Flowers are yellow, with spidery, strap-like petals; they appear on branches before leaves; sweetly scented. Bark is grey-brown.

KEY FACT
Japanese Witch Hazel has been cross-bred with Witch Hazel to create *Hamamelis* × *intermedia*, from which dozens of named cultivars have been raised.

STATUS AND COMMENTS
This species is a native of Japan, and its hybrids are grown widely in Britain for their flowers and autumn leaves. On wintry days, the sight and scent of the flowers can lift the spirits of even the coldest soul.

SPOTTER'S CHART

LOCATION	DATE/TIME

PITTOSPORUM (KOHUHU)
Pittosporum tenuifolium

SIZE Height to 15m **HABITAT** Gardens, parks; naturalised in mild areas **FLOWERS** May **HABIT** Upward-pointing branches when mature; more often seen as a shrub. Evergreen

IDENTIFICATION
Leaves are up to 5cm long; oblong and wavy, with wrinkly edges; shiny and dark green; carried on a purple-brown stem. Flowers are small (1cm long) and tubular, with purplish petals and yellow anthers; and strongly scented. Bark is dark grey and smooth.

KEY FACT
There are many Pittosporum cultivars, differing in shape and size, and with leaf colours that range from gold through greens to purple; many are also variegated. These cultivars tend to be less hardy than the true species.

STATUS AND COMMENTS
This native of New Zealand grows readily in mild areas of Britain, especially near the sea. It is a special feature of such places as the Isles of Scilly.

SPOTTER'S CHART

LOCATION	DATE/TIME

FACT FILE

SIZE Height to 30m HABITAT Parks, gardens, roadsides FLOWERS Apr–Jun HABIT Mature trees are massive and domed, sometimes with very spreading lower branches. Deciduous

IDENTIFICATION

Leaves are wider across than long (up to 25cm across); palmately lobed, with five to seven deeply cut lobes; glossy green above, paler below. Fruits are clusters of bristly spheres hanging on stalks. Bark is pale brown; smooth, but often flaking to leave creamy-yellow patches.

KEY FACT

Giant old Oriental Planes are dotted across (mainly southern) Britain. Some of these trees are very tall and many have huge trailing lower branches.

SPOTTER'S CHART

LOCATION	DATE/TIME

STATUS AND COMMENTS

Oriental Plane originates in the E Mediterranean and was once widely planted throughout Britain, although it lost out in popularity to the similar London Plane. Less frequent in the N and Scotland. An airy tree with elegant foliage.

LONDON PLANE
Platanus × hispanica

SIZE Height to 44m HABITAT Parks, squares, roadsides – many thousands in London! FLOWERS May
HABIT Long, straight trunk and dense, twisting branches. Deciduous

IDENTIFICATION

Leaves are up to 24cm long; palmately lobed, often with five main lobes; dark green. Fruits are very prominent and persistent spiky balls that hang on dangling stalks. Bark is grey, often flaking to reveal creamy-yellowy patches beneath.

STATUS AND COMMENTS

A vigorous tree that has become a city classic, probably always planted rather than naturally occurring. It resists pollution through frequent leaf renewal and by shedding its outermost bark in flakes.

KEY FACT

Its hybrid vigour (it is thought to be a cross between Oriental Plane and the American Plane or Buttonwood) means that the London Plane grows fast and lives long.

SPOTTER'S CHART

LOCATION	DATE/TIME

BRIDEWORT
Spiraea salicifolia

FACT FILE

SIZE Height to 2m HABITAT Parks, gardens; often a garden escape FLOWERS Jun–Jul HABIT Straggling, vigorous, ungainly shrub that suckers freely. Deciduous

KEY FACT

There are many cultivated varieties of *Spiraea*, some with very similar foliage and flowers. There are also at least three other brideworts, one charmingly called Confused Bridewort (*Spiraea × pseudosalicifolia*).

IDENTIFICATION

Leaves are dark green, elliptical and toothed (rather like those of a willow, hence its scientific name *salicifolia*). Flowers are a profusion of thick, garish pink wands; very short-lived, soon turning brown. Bark is reddish brown.

STATUS AND COMMENTS

Bridewort is native to a huge area, including parts of E Europe. In Britain it is an introduced garden plant, but can sometimes be found naturalised in the wider countryside.

SPOTTER'S CHART

LOCATION	DATE/TIME

QUINCE
Cydonia oblonga

FACT FILE

SIZE Height to 6m **HABITAT** Gardens, orchards; very occasionally in the wider countryside **FLOWERS** Apr–May **HABIT** Small and spreading, with a rather bushy appearance. Deciduous

IDENTIFICATION

Leaves are up to 10cm long; oval to elliptical; pale to dark green above, much paler and downy beneath. Flowers are pink. Fruit is often pear-shaped but may be rounder; when mature becomes golden and very aromatic. Bark is reddish brown.

KEY FACT
Quince fruits are highly and attractively scented but cannot be eaten raw; instead, they are traditionally used to make jelly. The cultivar 'Vranja' has very showy golden-yellow fruits.

STATUS AND COMMENTS

Quince (originally from W Asia) has been cultivated in British gardens for centuries, but it is not a commonly encountered tree. It is most likely to be found in town gardens.

SPOTTER'S CHART

LOCATION	DATE/TIME

FACT FILE SIZE **Height to 6m** HABITAT **Gardens, old orchards;
very occasionally in the wider countryside** FLOWERS **May–Jun**
HABIT **Small, shrubby, sometimes attractively bowed tree. Deciduous**

IDENTIFICATION
Leaves are up to 15cm long; lanceolate to oval, sometimes with fine teeth;
dark green, hairy underneath. Flowers are white. Fruit is very distinctive
and unusual: brown, up to 5cm long, with papery sepals still attached,
rather like a large rosehip. Bark is greyish brown. Good autumn colour.

STATUS AND COMMENTS
A native of SE Europe and Asia
Minor, the Medlar has long been
cultivated in Britain for its fruits.
However, trees are not very
commonly encountered and
are more likely to be seen in
S counties.

KEY FACT

The fruits can
be eaten only when they are on
the verge of rotting (a condition
called 'bletted'). At this stage they
can be used in preserves, or eaten
raw if you are brave enough.

SPOTTER'S CHART

LOCATION	DATE/TIME

WILLOW-LEAVED PEAR
Pyrus salicifolia

FACT FILE

SIZE Height to 10m HABITAT Gardens, parks, tree collections FLOWERS Apr–May HABIT Small, elegant tree whose appearance depends on the cultivar. Deciduous

KEY FACT The compact cultivar 'Pendula' has weeping branches and a dainty outline, and is very widely grown. Many consider this to be the most elegant ornamental pear, and it is the one you are most likely to see.

IDENTIFICATION
Leaves are very like those of willows: narrow, up to 9cm long and pointed at both ends; silver, becoming dark green. Flowers are white, opening with leaves. Fruits are small green pears, with sepals attached. Bark is very dark (almost black).

STATUS AND COMMENTS
Willow-leaved Pear is native to the Caucasus region and parts of Turkey. It is popular in Britain as an ornamental tree and its attractive looks make it ideal for small gardens.

SPOTTER'S CHART

LOCATION	DATE/TIME

PLYMOUTH PEAR
Pyrus cordata

103

FACT FILE

SIZE Height to 8m **HABITAT** Occurs very occasionally in West Country hedges **FLOWERS** Apr–May **HABIT** Small, slender tree, often little more than a shrub. Deciduous

IDENTIFICATION
Leaves are up to 5cm long but often much smaller; rounded, finely toothed; dark green. Flowers are white, opening with leaves. Fruit is a tiny round pear on a long stalk; brown at first, becoming red. Bark is dark brown, becoming plated with age.

KEY FACT This is one of Britain's rarest wild trees, restricted to parts of Cornwall and, as its name suggests, the area around Plymouth. It is nearly always found in hedges.

STATUS AND COMMENTS
Plymouth Pear has probably always been restricted to its natural range in Britain; it is more widespread in parts of France and the Iberian Peninsula.

SPOTTER'S CHART

LOCATION	DATE/TIME

WILD PEAR
Pyrus pyraster

SIZE Height to 20m **HABITAT** Hedges, woods
FLOWERS Apr–May **HABIT** Most likely to be noticed as largish, upright tree; easily overlooked when smaller. Deciduous

IDENTIFICATION

Leaves are up to 7cm long; rounded or elliptical, sometimes heart-shaped at base; glossy green above. Flowers are white, often covering tree in blossom as leaves open. Fruits are pears; yellowy green and very hard. Bark is dark brown. Branches are often spiny.

STATUS AND COMMENTS

This is now an unusual tree to encounter, but the many references to it in ancient land registers suggest it was once perhaps more widespread. It stands out only when in full blossom.

KEY FACT
The Wild Pear is very similar to the Common Pear, but the fruits are very different: while Common Pear fruits are appealing and highly edible in their many cultivated forms, Wild Pear fruits are definitely not.

SPOTTER'S CHART

LOCATION	DATE/TIME

COMMON PEAR (CULTIVATED PEAR)
Pyrus communis

FACT FILE   SIZE Height to 20m HABITAT Parks, gardens, hedges, orchards FLOWERS Apr–May HABIT Upright; old trees may be spreading and weathered; often pruned in cultivation. Deciduous

IDENTIFICATION
Leaves are up to 8cm long; oval or elliptical, often heart-shaped at base, usually toothed; glossy and leathery. Flowers are a mass of white, opening with leaves. Fruits are the pears we all know. Bark is dark brown, often with squarish plates.

STATUS AND COMMENTS
Originating in W Asia, the Common Pear is now cultivated almost everywhere. 'Wild' trees may have put themselves there or been left behind from a forgotten garden or orchard.

KEY FACT
Hundreds, or even thousands, of cultivars of the 'basic' Common Pear exist. Cultivation practices range from total neglect to extreme training and pruning, so looks differ hugely.

SPOTTER'S CHART

LOCATION	DATE/TIME

Pyrus elaeagnifolia

FACT FILE

SIZE **Height to 7m** HABITAT **Dry soils; uncommon**
FLOWERS **Apr–May** HABIT **Typically pear-like – upright
and slender – but often more like a shrub. Deciduous**

IDENTIFICATION

Leaves are up to 8cm
long; oblong, usually
toothed; woolly, greyish
white. Flowers are
white, carried in tight
clusters; appear with
leaves. Fruit is green
and may be pear-shaped
or round. Bark is dark
brown. Branches are
often spiny and twigs
hairy.

SPOTTER'S CHART

LOCATION	DATE/TIME

KEY FACT

This species is
included here to emphasise the
fact that many different pears
might be encountered in Britain,
both in cultivation and in the
wider countryside.

STATUS AND COMMENTS

This tree originates in the Near
East, and E and central Europe.
It is not common in Britain and
has no common English name.

FACT FILE
SIZE Height to 10m HABITAT Waysides and dry, sunny places; occasionally cultivated FLOWERS Apr–May HABIT Small, upright tree. Deciduous

IDENTIFICATION
Leaves are up to 7cm long; elliptical, not toothed; dark green above, grey below and woolly. Flower are clusters of white, appearing with leaves. Fruits are pear-shaped or round, becoming yellow with age; bitter. Bark is dark brown. Branches are often spiny.

KEY FACT Sage-leaved Pear is cultivated in areas (particularly in France) where perry is made and drunk, and where the bitter fruits add a depth of flavour to the drink.

STATUS AND COMMENTS
Not a common tree in Britain, the Sage-leaved Pear probably originates from central Europe. It may be a hybrid between the Common Pear and Snow Pear.

SPOTTER'S CHART

LOCATION	DATE/TIME

ALMOND-LEAVED PEAR
Pyrus amygdaliformis

FACT FILE

SIZE **H**eight to 6m HABITAT **O**ccasionally encountered in parks and arboretums FLOWERS **M**ar–Apr HABIT **S**mall tree that may become spreading with age. Deciduous

IDENTIFICATION
Leaves are up to 8cm long; oblong but variable, usually toothed; becoming dark green and shiny with age. Flowers are white and sometimes appear before leaves. Fruits are small and round, becoming yellow with age. Bark is olive-brown. Branches may be spiny.

KEY FACT

As with many of the unusual and rarely encountered pears, the name – in this case Almond-leaved – can be of help when identifying the tree.

STATUS AND COMMENTS
This pear is a native of central and SE Europe. It is not at all common in Britain, but might be found in some parks and specialist collections.

SPOTTER'S CHART

LOCATION	DATE/TIME

WILD CRAB
Malus sylvestris

SIZE Height to 12m HABITAT Woods, waysides, hedgerows FLOWERS May–Jun HABIT Small tree or shrub, basically conical in shape but can be very untidy. Deciduous

IDENTIFICATION

Leaves are up to 10cm long; oval, toothed; becoming shiny with age. Flowers are white or pinkish, opening from a pink bud. Fruits – apples – are small and green to yellow. Bark is dark brown. Branches may be spiny.

STATUS AND COMMENTS

The Wild Crab is native to Britain and much of Europe. It is a common tree in Britain, but is often overlooked.

KEY FACT

Crab-apple jelly is usually made from the many cultivated varieties of crab apples, but can just as easily (and tastily) be made from the Wild Crab. The little apples are impossibly sharp to the taste if eaten raw.

SPOTTER'S CHART

LOCATION	DATE/TIME

HUBEI CRAB
Malus hupehensis

FACT FILE

SIZE Height to 15m HABITAT Parks, gardens, arboretums, botanic gardens FLOWERS May–Jun HABIT Vigorous small tree with many branches, creating a spreading dome. Deciduous

IDENTIFICATION

Leaves are up to 10cm long; narrow and oval with a pointed tip; very shiny green when fully mature. Flowers are white, opening from a pink bud; produced in profusion. Fruits are small, deep red apples. Bark is reddish brown with scaly plates. Lower branches may almost touch the ground.

STATUS AND COMMENTS

A native of China, the Hubei Crab is widely planted in Britain, both for its wonderful display of white flowers and for its overall appearance as a handsome, shapely small tree.

KEY FACT This tree is one of the very many introduced to Britain in the early 20th century from China by the great plant hunter E.H. Wilson (nicknamed 'Chinese' Wilson).

SPOTTER'S CHART

LOCATION	DATE/TIME

FACT FILE   SIZE **Height to 8m** HABITAT **Parks, gardens, botanic gardens, arboretums** FLOWERS **Apr–May** HABIT **Small, neat, polite tree; often little more than a shapely shrub. Deciduous**

IDENTIFICATION
Leaves are up to 8cm long, elliptical, narrow, toothed, sometimes lobed; dark green and smooth above, downy beneath when young. Flowers, borne in great profusion, are white or flushed pink, opening from pink buds. Fruits are small yellow apples. Bark is dark brown and often fissured.

STATUS AND COMMENTS
This little tree has mysterious origins; it is thought to be a cultivated hybrid of two native Japanese crab apples, and was introduced to Britain as such from Japan.

KEY FACT

It is for its astonishing display of spring flowers that this tree is well known and loved. There may be so many flowers that the whole tree is covered in them.

SPOTTER'S CHART

LOCATION	DATE/TIME

SIBERIAN CRAB
Malus baccata

FACT FILE

SIZE Height to 15m HABITAT Parks, gardens, arboretums FLOWERS Apr–May HABIT Small tree with a spreading habit; less tidy than the similar Hubei Crab. Deciduous

KEY FACT

Like so many apple trees, the fruits of the Siberian Crab provide a welcome meal for wintering birds such as Blackbirds and other thrushes, especially as they remain on the tree for a long time.

IDENTIFICATION
Leaves are small and slender, matt rather than glossy. Flowers are bright white and fragrant, opening from pink buds. Fruits are small berry-like apples; green at first, becoming red or yellow. Bark is dark brown; not so plated as that of Hubei Crab.

STATUS AND COMMENTS
The Siberian Crab is a native of NE Asia; it was introduced to Britain in the early 19th century and is now quite widely planted here. There are a number of cultivars.

SPOTTER'S CHART

LOCATION	DATE/TIME

CULTIVATED APPLE (ORCHARD APPLE)
Malus domestica

SIZE Height to 15m **HABITAT** Parks, gardens, orchards; common in the 'wild' **FLOWERS** Apr–May
HABIT From large and untidy, to neat and polite if pruned. Deciduous

IDENTIFICATION
Leaves are up to 12cm long; oblong, rounded at base, toothed; rough and wrinkled to the touch. Flowers are white or pinkish, opening from pink buds. Fruits vary enormously in size, colour and taste, depending on the variety. Bark is dark brown and cracked when old.

KEY FACT
Cultivated Apple trees (especially old, rampant ones) are good for wildlife: the fruits are edible, the branches make good nest platforms, the bark shelters insects, and Mistletoe favours them.

STATUS AND COMMENTS
Cultivated Apples are found everywhere, and have been grown in Britain for hundreds (perhaps thousands) of years. Very many distinct cultivars have been developed here, with a range of intriguing names.

SPOTTER'S CHART

LOCATION	DATE/TIME

ROWAN (MOUNTAIN ASH)
Sorbus aucuparia

SIZE Height to 20m HABITAT Woods, waysides, mountains, moors; also parks and gardens FLOWERS Apr–May HABIT Small, often graceful and delicate-looking. Deciduous

IDENTIFICATION
Leaves are pinnate, with anything up to 15 pairs of leaflets, but more typically eight or so; each leaflet is up to 6cm long, sharply toothed, dark green above and grey-green below. Flowers are creamy-white plate-like clusters; scented. Fruits are clusters of bright red berries. Bark is silvery grey and smooth.

KEY FACT
The berries are a valuable autumn and winter food for birds, especially in wild countryside, where thrushes and Blackbirds often flock to them.

STATUS AND COMMENTS
Rowan is widely planted in gardens and in towns, but this native species is best seen in wild places such as moors, where its light character, grey bark and red berries add magic to the setting.

SPOTTER'S CHART

LOCATION	DATE/TIME

WILD SERVICE TREE
Sorbus torminalis

FACT FILE   SIZE Height to 25m HABITAT Woods, hedgerows,
especially in the S; very occasionally in cultivation FLOWERS May
HABIT A medium-sized, domed, neatly spreading tree. Deciduous

IDENTIFICATION
Leaves are up to 10cm long, with three to five pairs of toothed, pointed
lobes (tree can be mistaken for a maple); dark, shiny green. Flowers are
white clusters. Fruits are mottled brown blobs. Bark is brown, often
fissured into square plates.

STATUS AND COMMENTS
Uncommon these days, this native
tree is an indicator species of
ancient woodland. It was formerly
more widespread, as attested
by the number of pubs called
'Chequers' (the tree's old
English name).

KEY FACT
The 'Service'
part of the tree's name may
derive from the Latin for beer,
cerevisia, as an alcoholic beverage
was once made from the fruits,
possibly also reinforcing the link
with Chequers pubs.

SPOTTER'S CHART

LOCATION	DATE/TIME

WHITEBEAM (COMMON WHITEBEAM)
Sorbus aria

FACT FILE

SIZE Height to 20m HABITAT Woods, hedges;
also parks and gardens; prefers light and/or chalky soils
FLOWERS May HABIT Smallish tree with a narrow dome. Deciduous

KEY FACT
Whitebeam berries
attract a wide variety of birds in autumn
and winter, with members of the thrush
family finding them particularly tasty.
The name Whitebeam means 'white tree',
'beam' being the Saxon word for tree.

STATUS AND COMMENTS
Whitebeam is a fairly common
native tree of S downlands and
hedgerows, but is also widely
planted elsewhere. There are a
number of cultivars, including the
well-known silver-grey 'Lutescens'.

IDENTIFICATION
Leaves are up to 12cm
long; oblong, toothed
and with a pointed
tip; dark green above,
whitish and furry below,
with whole leaf feeling
rough. Flowers are
white, borne in small clusters.
Fruits are small red berries,
growing in clusters. Bark is
grey; usually smooth.

SPOTTER'S CHART

LOCATION	DATE/TIME

FACT FILE
SIZE Height to 7m HABITAT Restricted to parts of the West Country FLOWERS May HABIT Small tree or shrub, very similar in profile to Whitebeam. Deciduous

IDENTIFICATION

Leaves are up to 9cm long; oval, comparatively narrow, toothed, with small lobes on lower part of leaf; dark, shiny green above, grey-green beneath, and rough to the touch. Flowers are white clusters. Fruits are small orange-brown berries with many whitish dots (lenticels). Bark is greyish.

KEY FACT French Hales is also more understandably known as Devon Whitebeam – it can be found in a dozen or so known sites in Devon and a few in Cornwall, and also occurs in S Ireland.

STATUS AND COMMENTS

This is one of several very similar native species of the *Sorbus* genus that have very restricted ranges and are difficult to tell apart.

SPOTTER'S CHART

LOCATION	DATE/TIME

SWEDISH WHITEBEAM
Sorbus intermedia

FACT FILE

SIZE Height to 16m HABITAT Parks, gardens; often planted in towns and cities FLOWERS May HABIT Handsome, symmetrical, many-branched tree with a straight trunk. Deciduous

IDENTIFICATION

Leaves are up to 10cm long; elongated oval, with small serrated lobes that are deepest below middle of leaf; dark green above, pale green beneath. Flowers are white clusters. Fruit is a bright red berry. Bark is grey.

KEY FACT The lobed leaves help to differentiate this tree from the 'ordinary' Whitebeam, but note that there are several other members of the genus with similar leaves.

STATUS AND COMMENTS

This native of Scandinavia has been planted for a long time in Britain and is quite common here, perhaps especially in urban streets, where it tolerates dirt and pollution.

SPOTTER'S CHART

LOCATION	DATE/TIME

HUPEH ROWAN
Sorbus hupehensis

SIZE **Height to 12m** HABITAT **Parks, gardens, botanic gardens, arboretums** FLOWERS **May** HABIT **Small tree with vigorous, ascending branches. Deciduous**

IDENTIFICATION
Leaves are up to 15cm long, pinnate, with up to 17 leaflets, these partly toothed; distinct blue-green tinge, darker above and paler below; may turn deep red in autumn. Flowers are white clusters. Fruits are white or pink-tinged. Bark is purple-brown.

SPOTTER'S CHART

LOCATION	DATE/TIME

KEY FACT
The tree's very distinctive overall blue-green tinge makes it comparatively easy to recognise from a distance and is one of the main reasons for its popularity.

STATUS AND COMMENTS
Introduced from its native China in 1910 by plant hunter E.H. Wilson, the Hupeh Rowan is now grown quite widely in Britain. It is a good multi-season garden tree, but prefers deeper soils.

SARGENT'S ROWAN
Sorbus sargentiana

FACT FILE

SIZE **Height to 10m** HABITAT **Parks, gardens, botanic gardens, arboretums** FLOWERS **May–Jun** HABIT **Small tree with sturdy branches; may be as wide as it is tall. Deciduous**

IDENTIFICATION
Leaves are long and pinnate, with up to five pairs of narrow, oblong, toothed leaflets, these up to 5cm long; in summer, dark green above and furry beneath; in autumn, bright red. In winter, bears fat, sticky red leaf buds. Fruits are small red berries. Bark is dark brown.

STATUS AND COMMENTS
This species was discovered in China by the distinguished American tree specialist Charles Sprague Sargent, and introduced to Britain by the great plant hunter E.H. Wilson in 1908; it is uncommon today.

KEY FACT Sargent's Rowan is handsome in all seasons, but perhaps at its most glorious in autumn, when it bears plates of bright red berries and resplendent red foliage.

SPOTTER'S CHART

LOCATION	DATE/TIME

FACT FILE

SIZE Height to 5m HABITAT Parks, gardens, botanic gardens, arboretums FLOWERS Apr–May HABIT Small tree or shrub that tends to be bushy. Deciduous

IDENTIFICATION

Leaves are up to 5cm long; oval, toothed; light green in summer, dark red in autumn. Flowers are upright spikes of white blossoms with loose petals. Fruits are very dark blue or black.

KEY FACT

Numerous amelanchiers are cultivated in Britain for their showy flowers and varied foliage. Note that species names have changed, causing confusion; for example, this plant has also been known as *Amelanchier rotundifolia*.

SPOTTER'S CHART

LOCATION	DATE/TIME

STATUS AND COMMENTS

This native of Europe and Asia prefers mountain slopes and wild areas in its home territory; it is sometimes planted in Britain.

JUNEBERRY
Amelanchier lamarckii

FACT FILE

SIZE Height to 12m HABITAT Parks, gardens; sometimes naturalised in the S FLOWERS Apr–May HABIT Small, neat tree or shrub; domed and usually with a single trunk. Deciduous

KEY FACT Amelanchiers are grown for their delicate sprays of spring flowers, and for their foliage, which turns a spectacular range of reds and oranges later in the year.

IDENTIFICATION
Leaves are up to 7cm long; elliptical, finely toothed and with a pointed tip; purple-tinged, becoming bright green as they become mature. Flowers are white, with five petals; carried upright in sprays as young leaves open. Fruit is a purple-black berry. Bark is greyish brown.

SPOTTER'S CHART

LOCATION	DATE/TIME

STATUS AND COMMENTS
This North American plant is one of several very similar amelanchiers grown in Britain. Most prefer acid or sandy soils, but they will grow on chalky soil if it is not too dry or shallow.

HYBRID COCKSPUR THORN
Crataegus × lavalleei

SIZE **Height to 12m** HABITAT **Parks, gardens, roadsides** FLOWERS **Jun** HABIT **Attractive tree with a spreading outline; thickly branched. Deciduous**

IDENTIFICATION
Leaves are up to 10cm long; narrow, toothed towards tip; glossy green; they may stay on tree until winter. Flowers are white, carried in small bunches at tip of woolly stem. Fruit is a late-ripening orange-red berry. Bark is grey.

KEY FACT
The Hybrid Cockspur Thorn is perhaps most likely to be encountered in a town garden, or a town or city street or park. It is grown for its handsome shape and attractive foliage.

STATUS AND COMMENTS
This is a cultivated hybrid created in the 19th century between the rare Cockspur Thorn, from the northern USA, and a crataegus from Mexico, possibly *Crataegus mexicana*.

SPOTTER'S CHART

LOCATION	DATE/TIME

BROAD-LEAVED COCKSPUR THORN
Crataegus persimilis

FACT FILE

SIZE Height to 8m HABITAT Parks, gardens, streets, roadsides FLOWERS May HABIT Small, compact tree, round-headed when young, spreading when older. Deciduous

IDENTIFICATION
Leaves are up to 8cm long; oval, toothed; shiny green, turning varied reds and oranges in autumn. Flowers are white, borne in small sprays. Fruits are dark red berries (like hawthorn haws). Bark is brown and scaly. Even small specimens may have thorns up to 2cm long.

STATUS AND COMMENTS
This North American tree, or more likely a named cultivar, is commonly encountered in town and city streets, and in the countryside, where it is often planted as a hedge.

KEY FACT

The cultivar 'Prunifolia' is widely planted for all-year interest, from the spring flowers and bright young leaves, through to brilliant autumn colours of both leaves and fruit.

SPOTTER'S CHART

LOCATION	DATE/TIME

COMMON HAWTHORN
Crataegus monogyna

SIZE Height to 15m HABITAT Hedges, gardens, downland, moorland FLOWERS May HABIT Can be tall and straggly with dipping branches; often seen as a clipped hedge. Deciduous

IDENTIFICATION
Leaves are up to 5cm long; toothed at tip, with up to three very deeply cut lobes on either side; shiny green when young, pale underneath. Flowers are dense, bright white clusters. Fruits are dark red 'haws' containing one seed. Bark is greyish, sometimes with a reddish tinge.

STATUS AND COMMENTS
One of our most common and toughest native trees, often clipped to form a dense, thorny hedge and very widely planted in the past as a stockproof barrier.

KEY FACT
When in flower in May (hence its country name of 'May'), Common Hawthorn is a frothy mass of brilliant white flowers that give off a distinct and heady scent on sunny days.

SPOTTER'S CHART

LOCATION	DATE/TIME

MIDLAND HAWTHORN
Crataegus laevigata

FACT FILE

SIZE Height to 10m HABITAT Hedges, roadsides,
some parks and gardens FLOWERS May HABIT Often
encountered as a hedge, but also as a bushy tree. Deciduous

KEY FACT
Several cultivars of this tree are widely grown, including the striking 'Paul's Scarlet', which has deep red double flowers, and 'Rosea Flore Pleno', with pink double flowers.

IDENTIFICATION
Leaves are up to 6cm long; lobed and toothed (lobes are shallow in comparison to Common Hawthorn and teeth extend further down lobes); shiny green on upper surface, paler underneath. Flowers are usually white. Fruits are dark red 'haws', with two or three seeds inside. Bark is grey-brown.

SPOTTER'S CHART

LOCATION	DATE/TIME

STATUS AND COMMENTS
Midland Hawthorn is not as widespread or common as Common Hawthorn, even though it has been very widely planted in Britain. By nature it prefers heavier soils in woodland.

HIMALAYAN TREE COTONEASTER
Cotoneaster frigidus

FACT FILE

SIZE Height to 10m **HABITAT** Parks, gardens **FLOWERS** Jun–Jul **HABIT** Small tree or large shrub, often with several leaning stems. Deciduous or semi-evergreen depending on form

IDENTIFICATION

Leaves are up to 12cm long; oblong; leathery, dark green above, grey and furry below. Flowers are white clusters carried in dense upright heads.

KEY FACT

Self-sown cotoneasters putting themselves into sensitive environments in the wild are a worry to conservationists, but wild birds appreciate the heavy crops of winter berries.

Fruits are a profusion of large, dark red berries. Bark is grey-brown. Can have many very vigorous straight shoots.

STATUS AND COMMENTS

Many cotoneasters self-sow and readily hybridise, often thriving in difficult sites. In Britain, you are therefore more likely to see a hybrid of this native Himalayan tree than a true example of the species.

SPOTTER'S CHART

LOCATION	DATE/TIME

PEACH
Prunus persica

FACT FILE

SIZE Height to 8m HABITAT Gardens, walled gardens, glasshouses FLOWERS Mar–Apr HABIT Small, bushy tree; often trained against a wall. Deciduous

IDENTIFICATION
Leaves are up to 15cm long; narrow, elliptical, often folded, finely toothed, with a pointed tip; glossy dark green. Flowers are pink, opening before leaves. Fruit is the familiar reddish-orange peach, with velvety skin. Bark is dark grey.

STATUS AND COMMENTS
The Peach is native to China, and has been cultivated in Europe and Britain for centuries for its fruits. A number of cultivars exist, including some that are the smooth-skinned nectarines.

SPOTTER'S CHART

LOCATION	DATE/TIME

KEY FACT
Peaches can self-sow in Britain, often from discarded stones, but unless they are in a warm, protected situation the chances of them fruiting are very small. The leaves are prone to peach leaf curl, a disfiguring fungal disease.

FACT FILE   SIZE Height to 10m HABITAT Gardens, parks; virtually always in cultivation FLOWERS Mar HABIT Small, rather straggly tree, with an open, airy crown. Deciduous

IDENTIFICATION

Leaves are up to 12cm long, slightly wider than those of Peach and with a longer stalk; lanceolate, finely toothed, often folded lengthways, with a tapering point; dark green. Flowers are pink, borne in profusion before leaves emerge. Fruit is a small, furry oval. Bark is dark and blackish.

KEY FACT

Some varieties of Almond produce almonds (the seeds inside the stone) that are poisonous if eaten in appreciable quantities; only eat almonds from reliable sources.

STATUS AND COMMENTS

A native of the Mediterranean region, the Almond has been cultivated in Britain for centuries. It is generally grown in British gardens more for its flowers than its fruits.

SPOTTER'S CHART

LOCATION	DATE/TIME

APRICOT
Prunus armeniaca

SIZE Height to 10m HABITAT In Britain usually grown in protection FLOWERS Mar–Apr HABIT If free-standing is small with twisty branches; often trained against a wall. Deciduous

IDENTIFICATION

Leaves are up to 10cm long; rounded, with a pointed tip and often a flat bottom, finely toothed; tinged with red when young, becoming dark glossy green. Flowers are white or pink, appearing on stem singly or in pairs before leaves open. Fruit is oval, yellowish red, fleshy. Bark is reddish brown.

KEY FACT
Like many fruits, apricots are at their sweetest best only when fully ripe. They are best eaten sun-warmed straight off the tree. Some Apricot cultivars are grown for their flowers.

STATUS AND COMMENTS
This native of China and central Asia has long been cultivated in Europe for its fruit. In Britain, it usually needs shelter and care if it is to produce fruit.

SPOTTER'S CHART

LOCATION	DATE/TIME

CHERRY PLUM (MYROBALAN)
Prunus cerasifera

FACT FILE   SIZE Height to 12m HABITAT Gardens, hedgerows, waste ground FLOWERS Feb–Mar HABIT When mature, is an untidy but vigorous tree; more robust than other plums. Deciduous

IDENTIFICATION
Leaves are up to 7cm long; oval, tapering to base, finely toothed; shiny green. Flowers are bright white, appearing before leaves. Fruits are small, round red or yellow plums, soon falling when ripe. Bark is reddish brown. Has sparse, but very sharp, thorns.

STATUS AND COMMENTS
Introduced from the Balkans, this tree is surprisingly easy to overlook. It is most often noticed in late summer, when the trees have dropped a heavy crop of plums (although they do not produce a reliable crop every year).

KEY FACT
Cultivars such as the popular purple-leaved 'Nigra' and 'Pissardii' are grown for their early spring blossom (pale pink in purple-leaved forms) and ornamental foliage.

SPOTTER'S CHART

LOCATION	DATE/TIME

BLACKTHORN (SLOE)
Prunus spinosa

FACT FILE

SIZE Height to 6m HABITAT Hedges, woods, copses, thickets, waste ground FLOWERS Apr HABIT Untidy, straggly tree, often in suckered thickets, frequently in hedges. Deciduous

KEY FACT
The sloes, when well sweetened, are used in preserves, wine and to flavour gin, but beware the thorns – even scratches from these can cause painful localised septic infections.

IDENTIFICATION
Leaves are up to 5cm long; small, oval, tapering to base, finely toothed; dark green above, downy beneath. Flowers are white, often clothing entire tree. Fruit are sloes: small, hard, bluish-black berry-like plums; intensely sour. Bark is very dark brown – often black.

STATUS AND COMMENTS
A widespread native tree or hedgerow plant, once widely planted for hedging because of its impenetrable mass of intertwined, whippy branches. Can form dense, dark, very thorny thickets.

SPOTTER'S CHART

LOCATION	DATE/TIME

FACT FILE SIZE Height to 10m HABITAT Hedgerows, woods, gardens, orchards FLOWERS Mar–May HABIT Small tree with many slightly undulating branches; variable depending on form. Deciduous

IDENTIFICATION

Leaves are up to 8cm long; oval, tapering to base, toothed; dark green above, downy beneath. Flowers are white, or sometimes greenish white; carried in small clusters. Fruit is the familiar plum; variable in size and colour. Bark is reddish brown, but variable.

KEY FACT

Common Plums found in the 'wild' may tend to revert to characteristics of their parents: that is, spindly, thorny, and with small, unreliable fruits. Such trees are very often near to impossible to identify with complete accuracy.

STATUS AND COMMENTS

The Common Plum has been in cultivation for hundreds or even thousands of years. It was possibly originally a hybrid between the Blackthorn and Cherry Plum.

SPOTTER'S CHART

LOCATION	DATE/TIME

BULLACE/DAMSON
Prunus domestica ssp. insititia

FACT FILE

SIZE Height to 10m HABITAT Hedgerows, woodland edges, waste ground, old gardens FLOWERS Mar–Apr HABIT Small, straggly tree, often inconspicuous; sometimes very spiny. Deciduous

IDENTIFICATION

Leaves are up to 8cm long; oval, toothed; shiny green above, downy beneath. Flowers are white, sometimes tinged with green; carried in clusters. Fruit: bullace is round, either purple or yellow; damson is oval, purple. Bark is dark brown, becoming very dark red with age; fissured when old.

KEY FACT

These two escaped from cultivation long ago and make their own arrangements in the countryside, resulting in a mix of characteristics that can make identification all but impossible.

STATUS AND COMMENTS

Both Bullace and Damson are considered to be selected varieties of the Common Plum. They have much smaller fruits, but these are sweet when ripe, unlike sloes.

SPOTTER'S CHART

LOCATION	DATE/TIME

FACT FILE SIZE Height to 8m HABITAT Parks, gardens, orchards
FLOWERS Apr–May HABIT Small, rounded, shrubby tree
with a short trunk; may be surrounded by suckers. Deciduous

IDENTIFICATION
Leaves are up to 8cm long; oval or
elliptical, with a sharply pointed tip
and small rounded teeth; smooth
and shiny above, may be downy
beneath. Flowers are white, borne
in small clusters. Fruits are small
red cherries – edible but always
sour. Bark is reddish brown.

KEY FACT

'Morello' is a
well-known and widely grown
cultivar that is used in preserves
and cooking. It is often chosen
for training against a partly
shaded wall, and usually fruits
well without the need for
abundant sunshine.

STATUS AND COMMENTS
This native of SW Asia was probably originally a hybrid, subsequently
selected and cultivated for its fruits. It is grown in Britain, and can
sometimes be found in the 'wild'.

SPOTTER'S CHART

LOCATION	DATE/TIME

WILD CHERRY (GEAN; MAZZARD)
Prunus avium

FACT FILE

SIZE Height to 30m HABITAT Parks, gardens, hedgerows, roadsides, woods FLOWERS Apr–May HABIT Vigorous, handsome tree, with long, upward-spreading branches. Deciduous

KEY FACT Wild Cherry has long been cultivated for its fruits. In the countryside, birds (especially Blackbirds) devour those growing on unprotected trees long before humans have a chance to collect them.

IDENTIFICATION
Leaves are up to 15cm long; oblong or elliptical, tapering to base, with a pointed tip and prominent forward-pointing teeth; dark green above, paler and maybe downy beneath. Flowers are white. Fruits are dark red cherries. Bark is reddish brown with horizontal dotted bands (lenticels) and a tendency to peel.

SPOTTER'S CHART

LOCATION	DATE/TIME

STATUS AND COMMENTS
Common through much of Britain, where it is native. This is the sweet cherry grown in gardens and orchards; there are many different cultivars, many of them larger and sweeter than the species.

FACT FILE SIZE Height to 25m HABITAT Parks, gardens, hedges, roadsides FLOWERS Apr HABIT Rounded, open-crowned tree with long, ascending branches. Deciduous

KEY FACT

Sargent's Cherry is grown in Britain for its remarkable flowers, overall appearance and glowing autumn colours. Many think that this is the loveliest of all the cherries.

IDENTIFICATION
Leaves are up to 14cm long; oval to elliptical, with a sharply tipped point and small, sharp teeth; dark green and smooth above, pale beneath. Flowers are a very distinctive mauvish pink. Fruits (rarely seen in Britain) are blackish. Bark is purple-brown with horizontal lenticel bands.

SPOTTER'S CHART

LOCATION	DATE/TIME

STATUS AND COMMENTS
This tree is a native of the mountains of Japan. There are a number of cultivars, very often grafted onto a rootstock of Wild Cherry.

BLACK CHERRY (RUM CHERRY)
Prunus serotina

SIZE Height to 20m HABITAT Some parks and gardens; occasionally naturalised FLOWERS May–Jun HABIT Rather a straggly tree, with long branches that may droop. Deciduous

IDENTIFICATION

Leaves are up to 14cm long; oval to elliptical, with fine, forward-pointing teeth; dark, glossy green above, paler beneath with hairs along midrib. Flowers are white, carried on spikes. Fruits are small purple-black cherries; bitter. Bark is greyish brown, becoming fissured with age.

SPOTTER'S CHART

LOCATION	DATE/TIME

KEY FACT

The bitter aromas of this tree help to identify it. The cherries were once used to flavour rum, hence its alternative common name.

STATUS AND COMMENTS

This native of North America has been planted in Britain both for its timber and for ornament. It has become naturalised in some areas, particularly in the S counties.

FACT FILE   SIZE **Height to 15m** HABITAT **Parks, gardens, roadsides** FLOWERS **Apr–May** HABIT **Variable depending on form; often small with widely spreading, ascending branches. Deciduous**

KEY FACT   *Prunus* 'Kanzan' is one of the most popular cultivars derived from the Japanese Cherry; it has a mass of short-lived double pink flowers that turn rapidly to a soggy brown mess.

IDENTIFICATION
Leaves are up to 16cm long; oval to oblong, with a long, tapering tip and whiskery teeth. Flowers are white through to pink; often appear in great profusion. Fruits are rare in cultivated trees. Bark is dark brown. The species' many cultivars have widely differing characteristics.

SPOTTER'S CHART

LOCATION	DATE/TIME

STATUS AND COMMENTS
The introduced Japanese Cherry is hugely popular in Britain, for its many flower variations (including double-flowered) and overall tree shape and character.

YOSHINO CHERRY
Prunus × yedoensis

FACT FILE

SIZE Height to 12m HABITAT Streets and roadsides FLOWERS Apr HABIT Similar to the Japanese Cherry, but shorter and may be slightly weeping. Deciduous

IDENTIFICATION
Leaves are up to 14cm long; elliptical, with a very pointed tip and whiskery teeth; olive-green. Flowers are pink to white, with five petals; slightly scented; they appear in profusion before leaves open. Fruit is a small red to black blob. Bark is reddish brown with pronounced lenticel bands.

KEY FACT
Similar hybrid cherries include those described as 'weeping cherries', with pronounced weeping branches, and a wide range with pink flowers and differing habits.

STATUS AND COMMENTS
This Japanese hybrid is one of hundreds of ornamental cherries grown for their spring blossom. Yoshino Cherry and its many close relatives are among the most widespread in Britain, especially in amenity planting.

SPOTTER'S CHART

LOCATION	DATE/TIME

SAINT LUCIE CHERRY
Prunus mahaleb

SIZE Height to 12m HABITAT Parks, gardens, hedges; occasionally naturalised FLOWERS Apr–May HABIT Often a low, rounded shrub; can be a small tree. Deciduous

IDENTIFICATION
Leaves are up to 7cm long; rounded, sometimes with a heart-shaped base, small point at tip, finely toothed; glossy green above, may be downy beneath. Flowers are bright white, carried in distinctive sprays; scented. Fruits are tiny black blobs. Bark is greyish brown with rows of horizontal lenticels.

STATUS AND COMMENTS
This is a S and central European native, introduced to Britain early in the 18th century. Walking sticks and pipes were traditionally made from its wood.

KEY FACT

In Britain, Saint Lucie Cherry is usually grown for its flowers. Once the tree is established and a few years old, these are produced in fragrant profusion.

SPOTTER'S CHART

LOCATION	DATE/TIME

SPRING CHERRY
Prunus × subhirtella

SIZE **Height to 14m** HABITAT **Parks, gardens**
FLOWERS **Mar–Apr** (*but see* 'Key Fact') HABIT **In Britain, is a small to medium-sized tree with a dense crown. Deciduous**

IDENTIFICATION
Leaves are up to 6cm long; oval to lanceolate, markedly toothed, with a long-pointed tip. Flowers are pinkish white, opening before leaves (*but see* 'Key Fact'). Fruit (not often seen in cultivation) is a small black cherry. Bark is greyish. Twigs are a distinctive crimson. There are a number of forms, each with differing characteristics.

STATUS AND COMMENTS
Spring Cherry was introduced to Britain from Japan, where it does not occur in the wild. There are also very closely related forms that were introduced from the USA.

KEY FACT
If you see a cherry in flower during mild spells between Nov and Feb, it is most likely to be the Spring Cherry cultivar 'Autumnalis'. Other cultivars have pink flowers, such as 'Autumnalis Rosea'.

SPOTTER'S CHART

LOCATION	DATE/TIME

FACT FILE   SIZE Height to 16m HABITAT Open country, by streams, woods. Cultivated forms in parks and gardens FLOWERS May HABIT Medium-sized tree with slender, ascending branches. Deciduous

IDENTIFICATION

Leaves are up to 10cm long; elliptical to oblong, rounded at base, with a small pointed tip, finely toothed; dark green above, paler beneath. Flowers are white, carried on slender stems, either upright or drooping; scented. Fruits are shiny black cherries; very bitter. Bark is greyish brown.

KEY FACT

In late spring the scent of the flowers is a delight; many say it is reminiscent of almonds. The rest of the tree is found by some to have an unpleasant smell.

SPOTTER'S CHART

LOCATION	DATE/TIME

STATUS AND COMMENTS

Bird Cherry is native to parts of Britain, and is quite common in some areas. There are a number of cultivars (often introduced), including 'Colorata', with purplish foliage and pink flowers.

PORTUGAL LAUREL
Prunus lusitanica

FACT FILE

SIZE Height to 10m HABITAT Parks, gardens, woods, hedges, windbreaks FLOWERS Jun–Aug HABIT Most often seen as a dense, bushy shrub, but can become an architectural tree. Evergreen

IDENTIFICATION
Leaves are up to 12cm long; oval to elliptical, tapering to a tip, finely toothed; smooth, dark glossy green. Flowers are bright white, carried in masses on undulating spikes; fragrant. Fruits are red, then black, berries ('cherries'); inedible, bitter. Bark is dark grey-brown; smooth.

KEY FACT
Regarded as an excellent garden plant, providing shape, shade and shelter, Portugal Laurel is now problematic in the wider countryside, where it can spread fast and smother native vegetation.

SPOTTER'S CHART

LOCATION	DATE/TIME

STATUS AND COMMENTS
This native of Spain and Portugal was introduced to Britain in the mid-17th century. It is now widespread and common here, and thrives even on shallow chalky soils.

SIZE **Height to 10m** HABITAT **Parks, gardens, hedges, woods** FLOWERS **Apr** HABIT **Most often seen as a bushy shrub, but can become a medium-sized, spreading tree. Evergreen**

IDENTIFICATION
Leaves are up to 20cm long; oblong, with a bluntly pointed tip and random small teeth; smooth, leathery, glossy green. Flowers are white, carried on upright stems (much shorter than those of Portugal Laurel); fragrant. Fruit is a small cherry; red, ripening to black. Bark is greyish brown.

STATUS AND COMMENTS
A native of the Balkans that was brought to Britain in the 16th century, Cherry Laurel can thrive in even the densest shade and can smother all other plants around it. It prefers heavier soils than the Portugal Laurel, but does grow on chalky soils.

KEY FACT
Cherry Laurel contains appreciable amounts of cyanide, and the cherries should never be eaten. Some experts advise against pruning for the same reason; treat the plant with caution.

SPOTTER'S CHART

LOCATION	DATE/TIME

JUDAS TREE
Cercis siliquastrum

SIZE Height to 10m HABITAT Parks, gardens, botanic **FACT FILE**
gardens FLOWERS May HABIT Small tree with a spreading, twisty
character; often picturesque even when quite young. Deciduous

IDENTIFICATION
Leaves are up to 12cm long; very round, often heart-shaped at base,
sometimes with an indented tip; bluish green, becoming yellow later

in year. Flowers are a striking,
bright mauvish pink. Fruit is a
flat pod that stays on tree. Bark
is dark grey.

STATUS AND COMMENTS
The Judas Tree is a native of the
Mediterranean region and has
been grown in Britain for hundreds
of years. It looks at its best if seen
standing alone.

KEY FACT
No other tree
looks like the Judas Tree when
it is in flower: a mass of Sweet
Pea-like blossoms sprouts
directly from the shoots,
branches and trunk. Venerable
specimens often live out their
old age in the gardens of grand
houses around the country.

SPOTTER'S CHART

LOCATION	DATE/TIME

FACT FILE

SIZE **Height to 10m** HABITAT **Gardens, hedges; sometimes naturalised** FLOWERS **Apr–May** HABIT **Small, untidy tree with a thin trunk and upward-growing branches. Deciduous**

IDENTIFICATION

Leaves are composed of three elliptical leaflets, each up to 10cm long and with a slightly pointed tip; mid-green. Flowers comprise a hanging cluster of bright yellow pea-like blossoms. Fruit is a pea-like pod; seeds are green when young, ripening to black.
Bark is dark grey.

STATUS AND COMMENTS

Common Laburnum is a native of central and S Europe and has long been a popular garden tree in Britain. Similar species are the Scots Laburnum and Voss's Laburnum.

KEY FACT

All laburnums are highly poisonous, especially the seeds, which look very like peas when green. Voss's Laburnum develops fewer seedpods, and is therefore considered safer for growing in the garden.

SPOTTER'S CHART

LOCATION	DATE/TIME

FALSE ACACIA (LOCUST TREE)
Robinia pseudoacacia

SIZE **Height to 30m** HABITAT **Parks, gardens, arboretums** FLOWERS **Jun** HABIT **Mature trees are imposing, with spreading branches and a rugged-looking trunk. Deciduous**

FACT FILE

KEY FACT
True acacias include the Mimosa, or Silver Wattle, which has much more feathery/ferny leaflets and a mass of bright yellow feathery flowers.

IDENTIFICATION
Leaves are composed of up to 23 paired leaflets, each up to 4cm long and oval; pale green. Flowers are hanging clusters of white pea-like blooms; fragrant. Fruit is a dark brown pod. Bark is grey-brown; when mature, is rugged with deep, twisting fissures.

STATUS AND COMMENTS
A native of E USA, the False Acacia is widely planted in Britain, where it is often better known as the Locust Tree. The golden-leaved 'Frisia' is a popular cultivar.

SPOTTER'S CHART

LOCATION	DATE/TIME

FACT FILE   SIZE Height to 10m HABITAT Gardens; sometimes naturalised FLOWERS Jun–Jul HABIT Mature tree is small, with leggy branches; suckers are softly bristly and red-tinged. Deciduous

IDENTIFICATION

Leaves comprise up to 25 elongated leaflets, each up to 12cm long and serrated (overall leaf up to 60cm long); bright green, turning gold and red in autumn. Flowers are carried in largish, tight, elongated clusters. Bark is brown, rough; shoots are bristly/velvety, like antlers, hence the species' common name.

STATUS AND COMMENTS

Popular for its autumn colour and because it is easy to grow, this North American native is very vigorous, has an immense root system and suckers furiously. Very difficult to eradicate.

SPOTTER'S CHART

LOCATION	DATE/TIME

KEY FACT

When cut, Stag's Horn Sumach exudes quantities of sticky sap, which is an irritant, affecting some people seriously. All in all, it is not suited to most gardens, where it can rapidly become a pest.

FIELD MAPLE
Acer campestre

FACT FILE

SIZE Height to 20m HABITAT Hedgerows, woods, gardens FLOWERS Apr–May HABIT If free-standing, is a handsome, domed, many-branched small tree. Deciduous

IDENTIFICATION

Leaves are small, up to 10cm wide; palmately lobed, with five (sometimes three) lobes, the upper lobes with two rounded teeth and the two lower lobes smaller. Flowers are tiny, green; carried in tight clusters. Fruits are two-winged greenish-red 'helicopters' containing the seeds. Bark is pale brown and corky.

KEY FACT Like many modest and frequently overlooked British trees, the Field Maple is important for wildlife, providing food (fallen seeds) for small mammals and dense nest sites for birds.

STATUS AND COMMENTS

A British native, the Field Maple is common and widespread, succeeding particularly well on the chalklands of S and central England. It is widely admired for its golden autumn colour.

SPOTTER'S CHART

LOCATION	DATE/TIME

SYCAMORE
Acer pseudoplatanus

FACT FILE   SIZE **Height to 36m** HABITAT **Hedgerows, woods, cliffs, moorland, gardens, parks** FLOWERS **May** HABIT **Mature trees are large, domed, with a big crown and spreading branches. Deciduous**

IDENTIFICATION
Leaves are five-lobed, with deeply cut, ragged teeth; younger trees have much larger leaves (up to 26cm across) than older specimens. Flowers are pendulous yellow tassels among young leaves. Fruit is a pair of winged keys containing seeds. Bark is grey-brown, becoming fissured when old.

STATUS AND COMMENTS
The Sycamore grows everywhere, from the wildest and most inhospitable places to suburban gardens and inner-city waste ground. It is not always welcome. It was introduced to Britain from central Europe.

KEY FACT
Sycamore has a bad reputation because it self-seeds so easily and quickly, becoming a curse if left unchecked in native woodland. On the plus side, it does attract aphids, which in turn attract and feed wild birds.

SPOTTER'S CHART

LOCATION	DATE/TIME

NORWAY MAPLE
Acer platanoides

FACT FILE

SIZE Height to 30m HABITAT Parks, gardens, roadsides FLOWERS Mar–Apr HABIT Handsome, fast-growing tree, with a short trunk and large, spreading crown. Deciduous

IDENTIFICATION
Leaves are up to 18cm across; palmately lobed, with five to seven lobes, each toothed, lowest pair of lobes smaller. Flowers are lime yellow, carried in small, erect clusters. Fruits are paired green keys. Bark is grey, with small ridges.

KEY FACT Of the many popular cultivars of Norway Maple, one of the best known is 'Drummondii', with yellow-edged leaves (perhaps the most widely seen variegated tree). There are also purple-leaved cultivars, including 'Schwedleri' and 'Crimson King'.

STATUS AND COMMENTS
The Norway Maple is an extremely popular import from mainland Europe. It is planted all over Britain for its attractive shape, varying spring/summer leaf colours (depending on the cultivar) and bright autumn hues.

SPOTTER'S CHART

LOCATION	DATE/TIME

FACT FILE SIZE Height to 16m HABITAT Parks, gardens; prefers lime-free soils FLOWERS Apr–May HABIT Small, neat tree, often seen in shrub form; often in pots. Deciduous

IDENTIFICATION

Leaves are up to 10cm long and across; five to seven lobes, each lobe sharply toothed, but very variable according to cultivar. Flowers are red, borne on small, loose stalks. Fruit is double-winged. Bark is grey-brown. Has many cultivars with varying shapes and colours.

SPOTTER'S CHART

LOCATION	DATE/TIME

KEY FACT

The species shows huge variety according to the cultivar – members of the Atropurpureum group, for example, have large purple leaves. Many of the more delicate specimens are cultivars of *Acer palmatum* var. *dissectum*, such as 'Crimson Queen', with finely cut purple leaves.

STATUS AND COMMENTS

This native of Japan is one of the most popular small garden trees or shrubs, and is more likely to be identified by its scientific name rather than its English one.

DOWNY JAPANESE MAPLE
Acer japonicum

FACT FILE

SIZE Height to 10m HABITAT Parks, gardens, arboretums; prefers acid soils FLOWERS Mar–Apr
HABIT Usually a bushy shrub; remains bushy as a tree. Deciduous

IDENTIFICATION
Leaves are up to 13cm long and across; singular in shape, with up to 11 tapering, sharp-toothed lobes; downy when young, as are stems. Flowers are red, borne in drooping clusters on stalks. Fruit are two-winged keys. Bark is grey. Very variable depending on cultivar.

STATUS AND COMMENTS
A very popular and widely grown shrub or small tree originating in Japan, with many varying cultivars. These are grown for all-year interest and spectacular autumn colour in particular.

KEY FACT

Two popular cultivars are 'Aconitifolium', with deeply cut leaves that turn ruby in autumn; and 'Vitifolium', which has broad, fan-shaped leaves that shine in reds and golds in autumn.

SPOTTER'S CHART

LOCATION	DATE/TIME

FACT FILE

SIZE **Height to 30m** HABITAT **Parks, botanic gardens, arboretums, some gardens; prefers lime-free soils** FLOWERS **Mar–Apr** HABIT **Large, neat and domed. Deciduous**

IDENTIFICATION

Leaves are up to 13cm long; palmately lobed, with five lobes, whiskery tips only on main lobes; can be downy beneath, unlike Norway Maple. Flowers are small, yellow-green; carried in hanging clusters. Fruits are two-winged. Bark is grey, slightly rougher than that of Norway Maple.

KEY FACT As with most maples, the Sugar Maple is grown as much for its autumn colour as for anything else. The cultivar 'Newton Sentry' combines this quality with a remarkable tall, upright character to create a golden autumnal column.

STATUS AND COMMENTS

The leaf of this **NE North American** tree appears on the flag of Canada, and its sap is the most often used to make maple syrup of all the maples. It is not especially common in Britain.

SPOTTER'S CHART

LOCATION	DATE/TIME

SILVER MAPLE
Acer saccharinum

FACT FILE

SIZE Height to 30m HABITAT Parks, gardens, roadsides FLOWERS Mar–Apr HABIT Fast-growing tree with upwards-pointing branches; delicate-looking for a maple. Deciduous

KEY FACT Popular cultivars of this maple include *Acer saccharinum* f. *lutescens*, with orange-yellow leaves in spring; and 'Laciniatum Wieri', with pendulous lower branches and very pronounced leaf lobes. Both have fine autumn colour.

IDENTIFICATION
Leaves are up to 15cm long and across; palmately lobed, with five pronounced lobes, each of which is very sharply toothed; light green above, silvery beneath. Flowers are small greenish-yellow clusters. Fruits are two-winged keys. Bark is grey.

SPOTTER'S CHART

LOCATION	DATE/TIME

STATUS AND COMMENTS
A native of E North America and now widely planted in town parks and gardens in Britain, Silver Maple is a popular tree here but is said to be prone to breaking in strong winds.

FACT FILE   SIZE Height to 30m HABITAT Parks, large gardens; prefers lime-free soils FLOWERS Mar–Apr HABIT Fast-growing, ultimately large tree with a dense, cone-shaped crown. Deciduous

IDENTIFICATION
Leaves are up to 10cm long and nearly as much across, with three or five toothed lobes; dark green above, silvery beneath, turning red in autumn. Flowers are small, crimson; carried in dense clusters. Fruits are two-winged keys; red. Bark is grey.

STATUS AND COMMENTS
The Red Maple is a native of North America, where its fiery autumn colours are a vital part of the 'fall' (autumn). In Britain it is not quite so well known as other maples.

KEY FACT   Among the cultivars that display spectacular autumn reds are 'October Glory', 'Schlesingeri' and 'Red Sunset', the last with oranges as well as reds in its palette.

SPOTTER'S CHART

LOCATION	DATE/TIME

PAPER-BARK MAPLE
Acer griseum

FACT FILE

SIZE **Height to 15m** HABITAT **Parks, gardens, botanic gardens, arboretums** FLOWERS **May** HABIT **Small, neat, domed tree with unique peeling bark. Deciduous**

IDENTIFICATION
Leaves are up to 10cm long; composed of three distinct round-toothed leaflets; dark green above, very downy beneath. Flowers are green, small; carried in drooping clusters. Fruits are broad, two-winged keys. Bark is remarkable and very distinct, peeling away in paper-thin strips.

STATUS AND COMMENTS
A native of China, the Paper-bark Maple was introduced to Britain in 1901. The unique coppery-red and rich-brown peeling bark, and wonderful autumn foliage, make it an excellent garden tree, although it is not especially common.

KEY FACT
Brought back to Britain by E.H. Wilson, the Paper-bark Maple was the favourite discovery of this great plant hunter.

SPOTTER'S CHART

LOCATION	DATE/TIME
- - - - - - - - - - - - - -	- - - - - - - -
- - - - - - - - - - - - - -	- - - - - - - -
- - - - - - - - - - - - - -	- - - - - - - -
- - - - - - - - - - - - - -	- - - - - - - -
- - - - - - - - - - - - - -	- - - - - - - -

BOX ELDER (ASHLEAF MAPLE)

Acer negundo

FACT FILE

SIZE Height to 20m **HABITAT** Parks, gardens
FLOWERS Mar–Apr **HABIT** Fast-growing, rather untidy plant with
numerous shoots; often pollarded to keep it shapely. Deciduous

IDENTIFICATION

Leaves are up to 15cm
long; pinnate, with up
to seven leaflets, each
of which is irregularly
lobed (not obviously
maple-like). Flowers are
dangling tassels. Fruit is
a frail-looking cluster of keys.
Bark is greyish. Variable in look
according to cultivar.

KEY FACT

Popular cultivars of this
tree include 'Variegatum', with white
margins to its leaves; and, most popular of
all in Britain, 'Flamingo', with pink-edged
leaves. They are most often seen pruned
to create the best foliage effect.

SPOTTER'S CHART

LOCATION	DATE/TIME

STATUS AND COMMENTS

Widely planted in Britain, this
native of North America owes
its bewildering array of common
names to its resemblance to
Box (wood), Elder (leaves) and
Common Ash (leaves), rather
than to other maples.

HORSE CHESTNUT
Aesculus hippocastanum

SIZE Height to 30m HABITAT Parks, large gardens, hedgerows, streets in towns and cities FLOWERS May HABIT Tall and imposing, with spreading branches and a big crown. Deciduous

IDENTIFICATION
Leaves are very large; palmate, usually with five leaflets, each up to 25cm long. Flowers are colourful and showy 'candles': upright, pinky-white spires. Fruits comprise a spiny oval outer casing enclosing the familiar shiny brown conker. Bark is grey-brown. Also loved for its winter 'sticky-buds'.

KEY FACT
The English common name is said to derive from the ancient use of conkers in horse medicine, and from the superficial similarity between the fruits and those of the unrelated Sweet Chestnut.

STATUS AND COMMENTS
Originating in the Balkans, Horse Chestnut is one of Britain's most familiar trees. Most trees now suffer widespread damage by leaf-mining insects and/or brown fungal rusts, making them look prematurely autumnal.

SPOTTER'S CHART

LOCATION	DATE/TIME

RED HORSE CHESTNUT
Aesculus × *carnea*

FACT FILE   SIZE Height to 20m HABITAT Parks, large gardens, streets and roadsides FLOWERS May HABIT Large, handsome tree, but not so imposing as Horse Chestnut. Deciduous

IDENTIFICATION

Leaves are palmate, usually with five leaflets (generally smaller than those of Horse Chestnut), these often crinkled. Flowers are pink or red 'candles'; less conspicuous from a distance than those of Horse Chestnut. Fruit is oval or round, with few or no spines. Bark is greyish brown.

STATUS AND COMMENTS

This is a hybrid between the Horse Chestnut and North American Red Buckeye. It is commonly planted along avenues in parks and gardens.

KEY FACT

There are a numbers of cultivars, including 'Briotii', with deep red flowers; and 'Plantierensis', with pale pink flowers (although it is no good for small boys as it does not have conkers).

SPOTTER'S CHART

LOCATION	DATE/TIME

YELLOW BUCKEYE (SWEET BUCKEYE)
Aesculus flava

FACT FILE

SIZE Height to 25m **HABITAT** Parks, large gardens
FLOWERS May–Jun **HABIT** Visually a smaller version
of Horse Chestnut, often with twisting limbs. Deciduous

KEY FACT
Another buckeye that might be seen in Britain is the very similar and closely related Red Buckeye, also originally from the USA. As its name suggests, this species has red flowers.

IDENTIFICATION
Leaves are palmate, each leaflet up to 20cm long, widely spaced from its neighbour and more narrow and tapering than those of Horse Chestnut. Flowers are rather scrawny yellow 'candles'. Fruit is brown, spineless and pear-shaped, containing a conker. Bark is coppery brown.

STATUS AND COMMENTS
This native of the E USA is planted in Britain mainly for its autumn leaves, which are red. It is not especially common here.

SPOTTER'S CHART

LOCATION	DATE/TIME

COMMON HOLLY
Ilex aquifolium

SIZE Height to 20m HABITAT Woods, hedges, gardens, parks FLOWERS May–Jun HABIT Very variable: from a rounded but spreading tree to a neatly clipped shrub. Evergreen

IDENTIFICATION

Leaves are up to 12cm long; narrow, oblong, with very spiny teeth (except high up in mature trees, where often spineless); glossy green. Flowers are small, greenish white and fragrant (male and female flowers are on different trees). Bark is silvery grey.

KEY FACT

There are hundreds of Common Holly cultivars, differing in leaf colour and variegation, prickliness and overall tree habit. Many are garden favourites, as are several cultivars of the hybrid Highclere Holly.

SPOTTER'S CHART

LOCATION	DATE/TIME

STATUS AND COMMENTS

Common Holly is native to Britain and can be seen almost anywhere, the seeds spread by birds. Trees in big woods are often browsed by deer, creating a flat browse line.

SPINDLE
Euonymus europaeus

SIZE Height to 6m HABITAT Hedges, woods, waste ground; more common in the S and on calcareous soils
FLOWERS Jun HABIT Small, wavy, rather straggly tree. Deciduous

KEY FACT
There are several well-known garden Spindle cultivars, including 'Red Cascade', with big red fruits and scarlet autumn leaves. Other members of the genus include the evergreen shrub *Euonymus fortunei*, a native of Asia that has many commonly seen variegated cultivars.

IDENTIFICATION
Leaves are small, up to 10cm long; narrow, with tiny teeth; shiny green, turning browny orange in autumn. Flowers are tiny, four-petalled and greenish white. Fruit is a four-part pink capsule containing vivid orange seeds; poisonous. Bark is grey.

STATUS AND COMMENTS
Spindle is native to England, Wales and Ireland, and is common in some areas, the seeds spread by birds. Its hard wood was once used to make such things as skewers and spindles, hence its common name.

SPOTTER'S CHART

LOCATION	DATE/TIME

FACT FILE   SIZE Height to 6m HABITAT Parks, stately homes, gardens; occasionally in open countryside FLOWERS Apr HABIT A thickly leaved, bushy shrub; very often tightly clipped. Evergreen

IDENTIFICATION

Leaves are up to 2.5cm long; narrow, oblong, often notched at tip; dark and glossy above, paler beneath. Flowers are small, yellow. Fruit is a small capsule. Bark is grey. Entire plant has an indefinable smell, which some say is reminiscent of cats.

STATUS AND COMMENTS

Native to Britain, Box may have originated on chalky soils and is still occasionally seen on downland, as at Box Hill in Surrey.

KEY FACT

Popular as a hedging plant for centuries, Box can be clipped into almost any shape, including complex topiary. Unfortunately, it is now plagued by fungal diseases such as box blight, which can be exacerbated by clipping.

SPOTTER'S CHART

LOCATION	DATE/TIME

BUCKTHORN (PURGING BUCKTHORN)
Rhamnus cathartica

FACT FILE

SIZE **Height to 10m** HABITAT **Woods, hedges, waste ground** FLOWERS **Jun–Jul** HABIT **Straggly, bushy, shrub-like and slightly spiny; inconspicuous and easily missed. Deciduous**

IDENTIFICATION
Leaves are up to 6cm long; oval or rounded, with a pointed tip, small rounded teeth, and prominent veins on upper side; shiny dark green above, paler beneath. Flowers are green, tiny, fragrant. Fruit is a small black berry, often produced in large numbers. Bark is dark orange-brown.

STATUS AND COMMENTS
Buckthorn is a native shrub of calcareous soils, particularly in southern England; it is absent from Scotland. It is a foodplant of the Brimstone Butterfly.

SPOTTER'S CHART

LOCATION	DATE/TIME

KEY FACT
Buckthorn was used in traditional medicines for its powerful (and potentially dangerous) laxative and purgative properties – as one of its common names, and the second part of its scientific name, makes clear.

FACT FILE SIZE **Height to 5m** HABITAT **Damp woodlands, marshy places; on acid soils** FLOWERS **May–Jul** HABIT **Small; has thin, straight limbs when young, often becoming straggly. Deciduous**

IDENTIFICATION

Leaves are up to 5cm long; oval, with no teeth, prominent veins and a blunt tip; glossy green above, paler beneath. Flowers are tiny, greenish white, inconspicuous. Fruit is a small berry, beginning green, becoming red and then black. Bark is dark grey.

KEY FACT

Alder Buckthorn and Buckthorn are very closely related to one another, but Alder Buckthorn is found on acid soils, whereas Buckthorn is found on calcareous soils. The fruits of Alder Buckthorn are just as toxic as those of Buckthorn.

STATUS AND COMMENTS

Common in some areas – especially central England, parts of Wales and Ireland – the native Alder Buckthorn is absent from Scotland and much of S England.

SPOTTER'S CHART

LOCATION	DATE/TIME

SILVER LIME
Tilia tomentosa

FACT FILE

SIZE Height to 28m **HABITAT** Parks, gardens; frequent in towns and cities **FLOWERS** Jun–Jul **HABIT** Symmetrical, domed tree whose branches ascend from a straight trunk. Deciduous

IDENTIFICATION
Leaves are up to 12cm long; rounded, with a heart-shaped base, tapering to a sharp point, sharply toothed; dark green above, silvery white and woolly beneath. Flowers are small, yellow; carried in bunches; very fragrant. Fruit is a small hanging blob. Bark is greyish brown.

STATUS AND COMMENTS
Native to areas E of the Balkans, Silver Lime is quite widely planted in Britain, especially in town streets. Its lack of honeydew helps to make it popular.

KEY FACT
The nectar of all Silver Limes is narcotic and toxic to bumblebees, which drink at the flowers and then fall out of the tree. Honey Bees are not affected in the same way.

SPOTTER'S CHART

LOCATION	DATE/TIME

FACT FILE   SIZE Height to 30m HABITAT Parks, gardens; more
often in towns and cities FLOWERS May–Jul HABIT Distinctive:
massive, with a weeping outline and weeping branches. Deciduous

IDENTIFICATION

Leaves are up to 12cm long; oval or round, with a short tapering point,
toothed; dark green above, very silvery white beneath. Flowers are white,
small; carried in bunches. Fruit is a round blob. Bark is dark grey. The
bold, vigorous weeping habit is
a key identifier.

KEY FACT   This is a highly
regarded ornamental tree,
which is admired for its shape
and form, and for its excellent
autumn colour.

STATUS AND COMMENTS

The origins of this tree are
uncertain; it may have originated
naturally in the Caucasus, or it may
be a variant or cultivar derived
from Silver Lime, and correctly
known as *Tilia* 'Petiolaris'.

SPOTTER'S CHART

LOCATION	DATE/TIME

SMALL-LEAVED LIME
Tilia cordata

SIZE Height to 40m HABITAT Woods, ancient hedgerows FLOWERS Jun HABIT Conical when young; characterful when older, with burrs, shoots and interweaving branches. Deciduous

FACT FILE

KEY FACT Britain's biggest coppice stool (and one of its oldest) was discovered at Westonbirt Arboretum, Gloucestershire, by Dr Oliver Rackham. This Small-leaved Lime is 15m in diameter and at least 1,000 years old.

IDENTIFICATION
Leaves are small, up to 9cm long; rounded, with a heart-shaped base and pointed tip, finely toothed; dark green above, paler with tufts of hairs below. Flowers are very conspicuous: bright yellow, standing clear of leaves, and borne in profusion. Fruits are small brown blobs. Bark is grey.

STATUS AND COMMENTS
Botanist Dr Oliver Rackham has proved that this native species was the most widespread tree in Britain before Saxon times. Now it is used as an indicator of ancient woodlands, where it is most often found in coppiced form.

SPOTTER'S CHART

LOCATION	DATE/TIME

FACT FILE SIZE **Height to 40m** HABITAT **Prefers deep, lime-rich soils; also planted.** FLOWERS **Jun–Jul** HABIT **Tall, narrow, domed tree; does not have sprouts, unlike Common Lime. Deciduous**

IDENTIFICATION

Leaves are usually up to 9cm long (occasionally longer); oval, heart-shaped at base, with a pointed tip, toothed; dull green above, paler beneath and can be furry. Flowers are yellowy white, hanging below leaves. Fruit is a small, roundish woody blob. Bark is grey.

STATUS AND COMMENTS

This tree is probably native to a comparatively small area of Britain, centred around the Wye Valley in Gloucestershire, but has been very widely planted.

KEY FACT

There are several cultivars of Broad-leaved Lime (also known as Large-leaved Lime) that are grown for ornament. These include 'Streetwise', often used to create avenues of trees, and 'Rubra', known for its bright red shoots.

SPOTTER'S CHART

LOCATION	DATE/TIME

COMMON LIME
Tilia × europaea

FACT FILE

SIZE Height to 46m HABITAT Parks, large gardens, roadsides FLOWERS Jul HABIT Massive and imposing when mature; straight, with ascending limbs. Deciduous

IDENTIFICATION

Leaves are up to 10cm long and across; heart-shaped base, with a pointed tip, toothed; dull green above, paler and shiny beneath. Flowers are small, yellowish white, hanging. Fruit is small, woody, rounded. Bark is grey; trunk is often covered in a mass of sprouts and burrs.

KEY FACT Its amazing hybrid vigour has helped to make Common Lime very popular. It is planted everywhere, from city streets and squares (where its questing roots can cause problems to nearby buildings), to avenues, churchyards and farmyards.

STATUS AND COMMENTS

This tree is a hybrid of Small-leaved Lime and Broad-leaved Lime. It is very commonly grown, despite the rain of honeydew that falls from it from aphid infestations.

SPOTTER'S CHART

LOCATION	DATE/TIME

FRENCH TAMARISK
Tamarix gallica

FACT FILE

SIZE **Height to 8m** HABITAT **Windbreaks, hedges, seaside locations, gardens; not on shallow chalky soils**
FLOWERS **May–Aug** HABIT **Bushy and wavy. Deciduous**

IDENTIFICATION

Leaves are small (rather like cypress leaves), up to 2cm long, carried in sprays on whippy stems. Flowers are pink, tiny, carried in tight sprays. Bark is reddish. Very often seen looking windswept and untidy. Needs full sun to thrive.

KEY FACT

French Tamarisk is as tough as they come, able to thrive even on salt-laden, windswept beaches. It is used as a windbreak, and is also a common garden plant, where it is likely to be controlled by clipping.

STATUS AND COMMENTS

The species is common throughout much of Europe and may even be native to Britain, where it is particularly associated with SW coasts.

SPOTTER'S CHART

LOCATION	DATE/TIME

SEA BUCKTHORN
Hippophae rhamnoides

SIZE Height to 10m HABITAT Coastal regions, especially on the E coast; also in gardens FLOWERS Mar–Apr HABIT Small, thinly branched tree or shrub. Deciduous

KEY FACT
Because of its adaptability and attractive silvery looks, Sea Buckthorn is widely grown as a garden plant. The berries (which may be yellow on garden forms) often stay on the plant through the winter months.

SPOTTER'S CHART

LOCATION	DATE/TIME

IDENTIFICATION
Leaves are up to 6cm long, very narrow and thin; dull green above, with silvery scales beneath. Flowers are tiny; green on female tree, yellow on male. Fruits are orange berries on female tree. Bark is brown (silvery when old); shoots are covered in silvery scales.

STATUS AND COMMENTS
Sea Buckthorn is native to Britain, at least on E coasts. It has been planted on many other coasts as a stabiliser of sand-dunes.

FACT FILE

SIZE Height to 25m HABITAT Parks, gardens; also naturalised FLOWERS May–Jun HABIT Tall, wavy, many-branched; often grown as a coppiced plant in gardens. Evergreen

IDENTIFICATION

Leaves are of two sorts: juvenile leaves are up to 4cm long, round, stalkless, silvery blue; older leaves are up to 10cm long, elongated and sickle-shaped, grey-green. Flowers are small, white, carried in small clusters. Fruit is small (1cm long), cup-shaped. Bark is pink and grey; peeling.

KEY FACT

Many species of eucalyptus are now planted in Britain. Most have peeling bark, long, dangling leaves, and the familiar aroma. Many species are grown for commercial timber purposes, and this use seems likely to increase for biomass production.

STATUS AND COMMENTS

A native of Tasmania, Cider Gum is the most commonly planted eucalyptus in Britain. It is often bought for its attractive juvenile foliage, but if left unpruned can become a large, ungainly tree.

SPOTTER'S CHART

LOCATION	DATE/TIME

HANDKERCHIEF TREE
Davidia involucrata

FACT FILE

SIZE Height to 20m HABITAT Parks, gardens, botanic gardens, arboretums FLOWERS May–Jun
HABIT Slender, neat tree, with a conical crown. Deciduous

KEY FACT

The genus *Davidia* is named for Père Armand David, a 19th-century missionary, intrepid explorer and outstanding plant (and animal) hunter who discovered the Handkerchief Tree in a remote part of China. Another legendary plant hunter, E.H. Wilson, eventually brought the species to Britain.

IDENTIFICATION

Leaves are up to 15cm long; oval, with a heart-shaped base and pointed tip, sharply toothed; bright green above, pale and downy beneath. Flowers are made remarkable by two very large white bracts – the 'handkerchiefs'. Fruit is small, round; brown when ripe. Bark is orange-brown.

STATUS AND COMMENTS

This much-loved tree, introduced from China, is perhaps seen at its best in the setting of a stately home or park. The 'handkerchiefs' make it look as if it is covered in white bunting.

SPOTTER'S CHART

LOCATION	DATE/TIME

FACT FILE
SIZE **Height to 4m** HABITAT **Hedgerows, waste places, roadsides; prefers calcareous soils** FLOWERS **Jun–Jul** HABIT **Shrub-like and whippy; can form thickets. Deciduous**

IDENTIFICATION

Leaves are up to 8cm long; elliptical, with a rounded base and pointed tip; rich reds in autumn. Flowers are tiny, white; carried in bunches; scented. Fruit is a round black berry. Bark is grey; young shoots are often very red.

KEY FACT

Modest in every way, Dogwood belongs to the varied genus *Cornus*, which includes some of the prettiest and most useful garden shrubs and small trees. The features prized in different species and cultivars include variegated leaves, colourful winter stems, and even big, showy flowers.

STATUS AND COMMENTS

Dogwood (its name may be derived from 'dagger wood', as its hard wood was once used to make daggers) is a common – but often ignored – native plant, especially associated with S downlands.

SPOTTER'S CHART

LOCATION	DATE/TIME

CORNELIAN CHERRY
Cornus mas

FACT FILE

SIZE Height to 10m HABITAT Parks, gardens, botanic gardens, arboretums FLOWERS Feb–Mar HABIT Small tree or large shrub, with spreading branches. Deciduous

IDENTIFICATION
Leaves are up to 10cm long; oblong to elliptical, with a pointed tip; dullish green above, brighter beneath. Flowers are yellow, often covering entire (leafless) plant. Fruit is an oblong red berry (edible). Bark is reddish brown.

STATUS AND COMMENTS
Grown for ornament in Britain for centuries, *Cornus mas* (as it is better known to gardeners) is a native of S Europe and parts of Asia.

KEY FACT

It is the wonderful late winter flowers that make this plant so attractive for many gardeners, but one of its several cultivars, 'Variegata', also has brilliant white edges to its leaves.

SPOTTER'S CHART

LOCATION	DATE/TIME

FACT FILE

SIZE **Height to 20m** HABITAT **Parks, larger gardens**
FLOWERS **Jun–Aug** HABIT **Medium sized,
often broader than tall. Deciduous**

IDENTIFICATION

Leaves are large, up to 25cm long;
heart-shaped at base, wide in
middle and tapering to tip, with
prominent veins; fresh green,
lighter beneath and downy.
Flowers are prominent pinkish-
white 'candles'. Fruit is a long
(40cm), dangling 'bean', inside
which are inedible seeds. Bark
is greyish brown.

KEY FACT

As with so
many ornamental species,
this tree has several frequently
encountered cultivars, in this
case usually 'Aurea' (Golden
Indian Bean Tree), which has
large, velvety, soft yellow leaves.

SPOTTER'S CHART

LOCATION	DATE/TIME

STATUS AND COMMENTS

A native of the E USA (the 'Indian'
part of the name refers to Native
Americans), this tree is most
commonly seen in Britain in
parks and large gardens, where
its flowers and fruits make a
fine show.

RHODODENDRON
Rhododendron ponticum

FACT FILE

SIZE Height to 5m **HABITAT** Woods, moorland, parks, gardens; prefers damp, acid soils **FLOWERS** May–Jun **HABIT** Large, dark shrub-like tree, with snaking branches. Evergreen

KEY FACT
The *Rhododendron* genus contains many species and literally thousands of cultivars. Most of these are inoffensive compared to the rampant *R. ponticum*. Azaleas are often thought of as being separate, but they, too, are rhododendrons.

IDENTIFICATION
Leaves are large, up to 20cm long; oblong, leathery; shiny green. Flowers are pinkish mauve and bell-shaped, borne in large clusters. Fruit is a brown capsule containing seeds. Bark is reddish brown, scaly. Tree is often impenetrable when fully grown.

STATUS AND COMMENTS
This is the most common rhododendron in Britain (it originated in S Europe and Asia). It is the one most likely to be seen spreading through moorland woods, and is an invasive pest, shading out native wild plants.

SPOTTER'S CHART

LOCATION	DATE/TIME

FACT FILE   **SIZE** Height to 9m **HABITAT** Parks, gardens (forms woods in **SW** Ireland) **FLOWERS** Sep–Oct **HABIT** Small tree or shrub with a short trunk and dense, rounded crown. Evergreen

IDENTIFICATION

Leaves are small, up to 10cm long; oblong to oval, usually toothed; glossy dark green above, paler beneath. Flowers are creamy white, bell-shaped, carried in clusters; they appear at same time as ripening fruits from previous year. Fruits are red 'strawberries' (round, bobbly). Bark is reddish grey.

STATUS AND COMMENTS

Native to the Mediterranean region and to **SW** Ireland, this tree is widely planted elsewhere because of its attractive habit, pretty flowers and intriguing fruits.

KEY FACT

The 'strawberries' are edible, just, though they have little flavour – they are best used to make jam. Unusually for an ericaceous plant, the Strawberry Tree will grow happily on calcareous soils; it can also tolerate exposed conditions, but not extreme cold.

SPOTTER'S CHART

LOCATION	DATE/TIME

COMMON ASH
Fraxinus excelsior

FACT FILE

SIZE Height to 35m HABITAT Woods, hedgerows, open country, parks, gardens FLOWERS Mar HABIT Mature tree is large, elegant, shapely, open and airy. Deciduous

IDENTIFICATION
Leaves are pinnate, with up to nine leaflets, each up to 10cm long, toothed and with a tapering point. Flowers are tiny, opening from distinctive black buds. Fruits are 'keys' hanging in dense bunches. Bark is silvery grey, becoming ridged and fissured with age.

KEY FACT
Common Ash was often coppiced in the past (the wood has many uses), and ancient stools are among our oldest trees. As a firewood, Common Ash is unique in that it can be burned green, directly after cutting.

STATUS AND COMMENTS
Common, especially on calcareous soils. This is one of our most graceful native trees if allowed to grow to full stand-alone maturity. It can be remarkably fast-growing, and is quick to colonise open ground with self-sown seedlings.

SPOTTER'S CHART

LOCATION	DATE/TIME

MANNA ASH
Fraxinus ornus

FACT FILE

SIZE Height to 25m HABITAT Parks, gardens, streets FLOWERS May HABIT Dense crown (noticeably more so than that of Common Ash); spreading. Deciduous

IDENTIFICATION

Leaves are pinnate, with up to nine leaflets, each up to 10cm long, toothed, oval to lanceolate (wider than those of Common Ash). Flowers are creamy white, borne in prominent clusters; scented. Fruits are dense clusters of keys. Bark is grey to black; smooth.

KEY FACT The showy, fragrant flowers, attractive shape and pleasant autumn colour have helped to make this a popular ornamental tree. It takes its name from the sugary 'manna' that can be extracted from its sap.

STATUS AND COMMENTS

This native of central and S Europe and parts of Asia is quite commonly encountered in British town and city streets. It is sometimes called Flowering Ash.

SPOTTER'S CHART

LOCATION	DATE/TIME

COMMON PRIVET (WILD PRIVET)
Ligustrum vulgare

FACT FILE

SIZE **Height to 5m** HABITAT **Downland, wasteland, hedges; also planted** FLOWERS **May–Jun** HABIT **Low, spreading, straggly shrub, with arching branches. Semi-evergreen**

IDENTIFICATION
Leaves are small, up to 6cm long; oblong to lanceolate; shiny green. Flowers are white, carried in prominent sprays; fragrant. Fruits are small, round black berries; poisonous. Bark is reddish brown with vertical lines.

STATUS AND COMMENTS
This shrub is native to chalk and limestone areas of **S Britain**. It has also been widely planted, often as a hedge (*although see* 'Key Fact').

KEY FACT
The privet most often used in hedging is not this species but the Garden Privet, which has longer and wider leaves, and is more tolerant of non-calcareous soils.

SPOTTER'S CHART

LOCATION	DATE/TIME

COMMON LILAC
Syringa vulgaris

FACT FILE SIZE Height to 6m HABITAT Gardens; occasionally a garden escape FLOWERS May–Jun HABIT A small, untidy tree or large shrub; vigorous shoots and suckers. Deciduous

IDENTIFICATION

Leaves are up to 10cm long; oval and often heart-shaped; dark green and waxy in appearance. Flowers are lilac-coloured, carried in large, fragrant cones; prone to frost damage. Bark is light brown, becoming shallowly fissured with age.

STATUS AND COMMENTS

Native to the Balkans, Common Lilac has been planted for ornament throughout Europe for centuries. It suckers freely, and has become naturalised in some areas of Britain.

KEY FACT

There are many cultivars of Common Lilac, with flower colours ranging from the traditional lilac to wine-red (in the well-known 'Souvenir de Louis Späth'), purple, pure white, and even primrose yellow.

SPOTTER'S CHART

LOCATION	DATE/TIME

ELDER
Sambucus nigra

SIZE Height to 10m HABITAT Hedgerows, woods, wasteland, gardens FLOWERS May–Jul HABIT Often bushy; sometimes tall and inelegant, with wavy branches. Deciduous

IDENTIFICATION
Leaves comprise up to five leaflets, each up to 12cm long, oval, with a pointed tip, toothed. Flowers are white, carried in large, flat, impressive clusters; fragrant. Fruits are purple-black berries, produced in large bunches; poisonous if eaten raw. Bark is grey-brown; gnarled and fissured in old trees.

KEY FACT
Elder gets a bad press, often derided as a weed and because some people don't like its musky scent. But the flowers make delicious cordials and the berries make fine wine. It is good for birds and insects, too.

STATUS AND COMMENTS
Very common and widespread native. It does especially well on richer soils, for example where Rabbits are numerous – they don't eat it, but manure it with their droppings.

SPOTTER'S CHART

LOCATION	DATE/TIME

FACT FILE

SIZE Height to 4m HABITAT Damp woods, hedgerows, waste places, stream-sides FLOWERS Jun–Jul HABIT Bushy, somewhat spreading, small shrub-like tree. Deciduous

IDENTIFICATION

Leaves are up to 8cm long, with three (sometimes five) pronounced lobes, irregularly toothed. Flowers are pure white, grouped in prominent, circular plates. Fruits are bright red berries, in bunches. Bark is reddish brown.

STATUS AND COMMENTS

The native Guelder Rose is common where the soil meets its requirements: moist, rich and chalky for preference. It is commonly grown in gardens for its flowers, fruits and autumn colours.

KEY FACT

The glistening red berries remain on the plant after the leaves have fallen, sometimes eventually attracting flocks of hungry birds in late winter, including migrants such as Fieldfares and Redwings.

SPOTTER'S CHART

LOCATION	DATE/TIME

WAYFARING TREE
Viburnum lantana

SIZE Height to 6m **HABITAT** Hedges, woodland edges, downs, scrub; chalky soils **FLOWERS** May–Jul **HABIT** Small tree or shrub; spreading, not tidy. Deciduous

IDENTIFICATION

Leaves are up to 14cm long; oval, toothed, rough; bright green above, furry beneath. Flowers are white, grouped in prominent rounded plates. Fruits are berries, in bunches: red and black together. Bark is brown.

KEY FACT

Wayfaring Tree may take its name from the fact that is was found by the side of remote country lanes, and happened upon by wayfarers in such places. It sometimes has a dusty look, as if coated from the chalky tracks by which it grows.

STATUS AND COMMENTS

This little tree, native to S England and S Wales, is particularly characteristic of the downs of S England, where its white flowers brighten up hedgerows and open country in the late spring and early summer.

SPOTTER'S CHART

LOCATION	DATE/TIME

FACT FILE

SIZE Height to 7m HABITAT Parks, gardens;
occasionally in hedges FLOWERS Jan–Apr
HABIT Large, dense shrub with glossy foliage. Evergreen

IDENTIFICATION

Leaves are up to 10cm long, oval; dark and glossy above, paler beneath.
Flowers are white with pink buds, carried in open clusters. Fruit is small,
egg-shaped; metallic blue,
becoming black. Bark is brown.

STATUS AND COMMENTS

A native of the Mediterranean,
Viburnum tinus, as gardeners may
know it better, has been cultivated
in Britain since the late 16th
century, and is among the most
widely grown evergreen shrubs,
popular for its winter flowers.

KEY FACT

There are
many Laurustinus cultivars,
including 'Purpureum', with
bronze-tinged growth; 'French
White', with showy white
flowers; and 'Eve Price', a more
compact form.

SPOTTER'S CHART

LOCATION	DATE/TIME

INDEX

PHOTOGRAPHIC ACKNOWLEDGEMENTS

Photographs supplied by Nature Photographers Ltd. All photographs by Paul Sterry except for the those on the following pages:

Frank Blackburn: 90; Brinsley Burbidge 154; Kevin Carlson: 63, 155; Andrew Cleave: 8, 12, 13, 16, 22, 36, 56, 57, 75, 77, 122, 123, 137, 146, 149, 152, 157, 175; David Rae: 140; Roger Tidman: 136.